Apr 28 '05

Mary—

To entice you to
return to Africa —
when you don't have to
worry about Mise I.

Warmest regards,

Jean Peter + Michael

Todd

Malawi
the warm heart of africa

Photography by Frank Johnston
Text by Sandy Ferrar

Central Africana Limited
Blantyre, Malawi, 2002

First published by Central Africana Limited, P.O. Box 631, Blantyre, Malawi October 2002
© Central Africana Limited 2002

ISBN 99908 14 11 2

Design and Typesetting by Arden House Design
Colour reproduction by Unifoto
Printed by Hansa Reproprint
Bound by Graphicraft

Publisher's Introduction

We were as surprised as anyone else at the popularity of our last major book on Malawi, *Lake of Stars*. It ran to three printings and nearly 10000 copies. And that despite a content restricted to our beautiful lake and the lakeshore.

Nevertheless, while it was in print, it became obvious that, for our visitors who did not visit the Lake, and the many residents who could appreciate the diverse beauty of Malawi away from the littoral, a more comprehensive photographic coverage of Malawi was required.

That remained a dream until I met Sandy Dacombe. For years she had worked in radio and was then in Lilongwe, working as an independent journalist with her own website and electronic newsletter devoted to Malawi and Africa. She was especially concerned with environmental aspects of the continent's issues of the day. Her powers of descriptive writing were and remain unusually vivid. Her work here makes more accessible, and to a greater number of readers, Malawi, its people, wildlife and scenery. It also brings these subjects to colourful life in a way that my own photography was sometimes destined never to do. The wrong time of year, of the day, inclement weather, poor light, all of these can conspire to defeat the most enthusiastic and patient photographer of the plethora of Malawi's scenic attractions.

The book is still not comprehensive in its coverage and we are very aware of what is not included. The Lake section was deliberately held back in length - with a view to a revised edition of *Lake of Stars*. Many other aspects are omitted in favour of a small selection of places and themes which we felt to be of real interest to the intelligent visitor and Malawian resident. The arts and culture in Malawi today are also not given the coverage this aspect of the country so deserves but they will be the subject of several other titles in the next two or three years.

Tourism remains a highly enigmatic subject in Malawi, the country having to date essentially failed to attract in numbers the international tourists it so needs and deserves. It seems significant then that such tourism success as we have had has been achieved in the hands of bold foreign entrepreneurs. They see clearly Malawi's tourist appeal and potential as we who live and work here never quite seem to appreciate. In many cases they have created quite exceptional small scale tourism developments perfectly attuned to market demand. In this book we have featured them wherever we have learned of them, and hope that the little publicity accorded them will bring them further success and encourage them to even greater effort.

I owe an enormous debt of gratitude to my long-suffering wife Maria Ines and our family. When not plainly absent in Cape Town working on this or other book design I could be found at Chintheche by the shores of this most beautiful of lakes, working early morning hours in pursuit of the perfect dawn photograph.

Hopefully the reader will enjoy this book as much as I have enjoyed creating it!

Frank M I Johnston
Chintheche, Lake Malawi
October 2002

Contents

The warmth of the heart

Many years ago the man who took the photographs in this book coined the phrase, *the Warm Heart of Africa* to describe Malawi. Certainly it was a marketing ploy, and like most sales gimmicks, it took a while to catch on. Now it's become so much a part of our thinking that it's hard to imagine any other way to describe Malawi. What makes it so successful is its surprising truth. Not that Malawi is geographically at the heart of Africa, but that its people epitomise all the gentle, joyful, forgiving and laughter-filled traits of Africans. The people of Malawi are the real warmth of this heart.

Malawi is not a wealthy country, but there are great riches in the people. These are the most polite, patient and friendly folk you are ever likely to meet. Their peace-loving nature fosters a need to please, and often their personal sensitivity towards a stranger makes them seem almost psychic. As a crowd, their sense of humour overcomes their sensitivity, and a discomforting moment, like a collapsing chair, is greeted with joyful hilarity. Malawians might have invented retail therapy, since buying and selling is, to them, not so much an economic exchange as an essential social transaction.

The loyalty of Malawians is proverbial. A friend tells the story of a visit to Ntcheu prison, which was enclosed by a feeble knee-high fence of barbed wire. He enquired about the frequency of break-outs, and was told, "Ah, no! Our prisoners here are very loyal." The story may be apocryphal, but Malawian loyalty is not. One need look no further than the fact that as an ex-colonial independent state, Malawi still honours the man who initiated colonisation. Dr David Livingstone is commemorated in Blantyre, named for his birthplace, the motor vessel *Ilala* still remembers the place of his death, and the name Livingstonia continues to celebrate his concern for the people of this country. These have not undergone the Afro-centric name changes considered inevitable in an emergent country.

Admittedly, Livingstone was an extraordinary man. If the Victorian British public took him to their hearts as a missionary explorer / hero and modest family man, the Africans saw him as a saviour, a man of iron will and unflinching bravery, a medical man who gave his life for the betterment of the African. Today we know he was far more complex than these idealistic views, but despite our ability to view him with the clarity of hind-sight and the honesty of distance, Livingstone

still imbues Malawi with his own distinctive flavour of high adventure and romance.

With your eyes crinkled against the dancing light from Livingstone's "lake of stars", you can almost catch a glimpse of the figure in a three piece, blue serge suit despite the heat, hands on hips, peaked cap squarely set, walrus moustache bristling irritably. Always he seems alone. Perhaps great men always are. It's surprising that he looks so slight; a small man, really. Remarkable that the three men who stand head and shoulders above the rest in Malawi's history were all physically small.

One of the most remarkable people Malawi has ever known was a diminutive chubby-faced fellow with handle-bar moustaches and a voracious appetite for knowledge. His name was Harry Hamilton Johnston, and, in 1891 when he was only 32, he became the first British Commissioner and Consul-General of what was then Nyasaland. More recently described as "... five foot three inches of demonic energy and ambition", Johnston changed the face of the country within five years.

Those five years were hardly a stroll in the park. Johnston - a trained artist - established just under 400 miles of roads suitable for wheeled traffic where he had found only one, and erected roughly forty administrative *bomas* throughout the country. He established a central government maintaining law, order and defence; a medical service was begun; a postal system instituted, and hut taxes and revenue collection made the administration almost self-supporting.

One wonders what a Victorian artist could have known about warfare. Yet in those five years Sir Harry Johnston broke the rampant slave trade around Lake Nyasa. That alone demands huge respect. But Johnston did more. He established administrative posts in North-Eastern Rhodesia at the same time. He named our area British Central Africa and - presumably on those long, dark tropical nights, working by candle or paraffin lamp - wrote his *Report on the First Three Years' Administration of the Eastern Portion of British Central Africa..*

He was a very knowledgeable man with a lively imagination and a flair for descriptive writing. There is a charming, typically Victorian, flavour to his writing and his encyclopaedic work *British Central Africa*, first published in 1897, was still being reprinted in 1969.

Lavishly illustrated with his own impeccable paintings, drawings and etchings, not to mention that technological innovation the photograph, this vast tome is about as thorough as a single book can get. It contains a staggering assortment of knowledge and research. I wonder if Harry Hamilton Johnston was an insomniac. Perhaps his journals and paintings were a therapy to counterbalance dealing with recalcitrant Arab slave traders, treacherous colluding chieftains and fractious European missionaries and planters. He claimed to have had more trouble from the Europeans than he ever had from the local populace.

*Opposite: Livingstone greets the local
people - the stained glass window
at Livingstonia*

*St Michael and all Angels in Blantyre
is one of many churches throughout
Malawi which were built as a direct
result of Livingstone's dedication
and perseverance*

*An etching of the famous missionary
explorer in 1857*

The arrival of the missionaries and the traders brought an immediate need for improved communications and transport

The African Lakes Corporation was quick to supply a fleet of paddle and other steamers on the River access route and on the Lake itself

Any man with this amount of ability and drive must be difficult to live with. Sir Harry was, to some, impossible. Besides, he was an odd little fellow. Contemporary descriptions mention his high and squeaky voice, his effete manner, his extreme vanity. We are told he was petty, lacking in both presence and dignity, an eccentric dresser and prone to "scream if a moth settled on him." But there are equally as many references to his charm, his intelligence and interest, his enthusiasm and tirelessness at work. He was said to be a genial spirit, a good fellow, a man who had a way with words, and "a very real influence ... over almost every person with whom he came into contact."

His photographs show only one side of this complex man. He looks for all the world like a nine-year old schoolboy wearing a false moustache and a silly expression. This is the leader who was unperturbed by warlike chiefs, murderous slavers and fierce beasts, and the simpering Victorian who wrote with distaste about "malicious vegetation".

The third colossus was, like Livingstone, a medical doctor from humble origins and a devout Christian. Once described as "the gnomish little doctor with the foppish clothes", Hastings Kamuzu Banda seems an equally unlikely hero for an emerging country. Like Livingstone, much can (and has) been said in praise and in condemnation of Dr Banda. His leadership of the country was a benign dictatorship, and it depends on your own political bent where you place the emphasis. Certainly he forced Malawi into unity, and fiercely maintained the infrastructure of the country. "Things worked

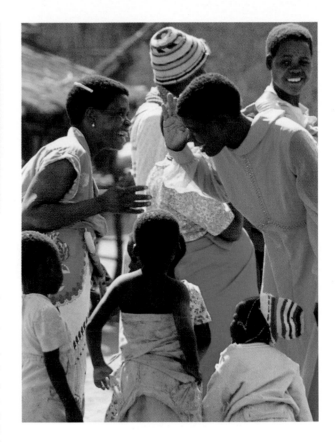

in Banda's day," you will often be told. "Ah, but we had no freedom!" will come the immediate response.

Think of Banda, and you can think of all the repressions imposed on individuals. Mens' hair had to be of a regulation length, not more, and women were not allowed to show their legs, even covered by trousers. Men were allowed to wear bell bottoms, the height of male fashion in the first half of the seventies, but the width at the ankle had to be no more than six fifths of that at the knee. It seems the real purpose of this bizarre law was to ensure that no lascivious bulges might tempt the women from their presumed virtue, since at that time trousers which were tight-fitting tended to have bell bottoms!

Any non-Malawian who even implied a criticism or disrespect toward Dr Banda was immediately expelled from the country. The closure of the Goan Club for some perceived infringement of the rules prohibiting music on Martyr's Day is still remembered with distaste. And there were much worse repressions; political adversaries were thrown in jail or simply disappeared. Nevertheless, like or loathe him, Kamuzu achieved as much as Harry Johnston in pure administration; under Banda Malawi became a modern, and a financially, as much as politically, independent country.

Malawi, in fact, seems to straddle time. In rural areas, life continues much as it did centuries ago: the men will hunt perhaps, or fish; women will draw water, hoe the fields, pound grain or cassava into meal, gather indigenous plants for relishes or cures. If there is too little to go round, as is

increasingly the case in years of erratic rainfall, the men will go in search of work, and come face to face with another Malawi. A Malawi with a fibre-optic telephone system, digital television, cell phones and CD players, lap-top computers and internet links. It's astounding how serenely people cope with this welter of technology when for many, piped water, electricity and private motor cars are still luxuries and the stuff of day-dreams.

Poaching has reduced some wildlife areas to almost empty tracts of bush, yet people outside of the parks still experience the terrors of wild Africa. In 2002 alone, elephants raided crops in Phirilongwe, a woman was killed by lions on the road between Kasungu and Nkhotakota, and several

The Highlands above the Lake around Dedza become magnificent fields of flowers when the cosmos bloom in May

Yao initiates by the lakeshore

The Cultural Museum at Mua Mission, far right, preserves Malawi's wonderful cultural heritage

children were taken by hyenas near Blantyre. Crocodiles frequently snatch fishermen along the Shire River, and occasionally people are killed by hippos on the lake shore. For a fortunate few, this is part of the excitement of living in Central Africa, but for the less-well-insulated, these are appalling daily terrors. It's unlikely that these last points of conflict between man and nature will endure much longer, but while they do, we are caught in a time warp between ancient Africa and the age of information technology.

Malawi still has those links with the past that are so easily lost with urbanisation, the social traditions of the people. Grass skirted Yao initiates, or the Zinyau participants in the Great Dance, the *Gule Wamkulu*, can still be glimpsed now and then as we scurry between cities conducting our international business, and Angoni warriors celebrate their descent from the Ngoni tribes of southern Africa, the arrogant and warlike Zulu. Besides being preserved for posterity in the marvellously unique cultural museum at Mua, these are still living rites-of-passage, shifting subtly to adapt to the current pressures of life. They are thrilling enough to attract the attention of tourists, and it is to be hoped that the spiritual heritage will not be eroded and debased as so many traditional dances have been elsewhere in the developing world.

It seems, though, that despite Malawi's multiple attractions, its endowment with so many tourism possibilities, that the industry has huge barriers to overcome. Malawi still appears to have no understanding of how appealing Malawi is, of

what is attractive to visitors, nor how to make the most of these assets. Given the threatened tobacco market, more effort could easily be put into really getting to grips with how tourism works, what international visitors would like to experience or how to reach key markets.

Malawi's loveliness touches the heart. Landlocked and isolated by rugged terrain, it has a balmy year-round climate and wonderfully fertile and productive land. It once had tall forests of beautiful trees as far as the eye could see, and the Lake was a magic pot producing endless quantities of fish and sparkling fresh water. Its very isolation afforded some protection. It was a fecund, flourishing little paradise, and in many ways, it still is. It's hardly surprising, then, that Malawi has one of the highest population densities in Africa. Tourism could be the goose that lays the golden egg for our country, but as long as we continue to eat the goose, we will all get steadily poorer.

In the meantime, Malawi remains a mostly undiscovered African jewel. The name is said to refer to "reflected light". Some feel this means the burning light from the lake, some think it's the reflected fire of dawn, others that it refers to the glow reflected from iron smelting kilns at night, for the original Amaravi were great iron workers. Whatever the actual etymological origin, the resonance is perfect. In winter you see the distance fade into thick, smoke laden air as the grass fires dance through the hills, and sunlight is trapped and reflected in the milky haze. At night, glowing necklaces of advancing flames lie on the breasts of hills and paint the rising smoke ruby and amber. In the summer wet season, rain-rinsed skies provide sudden superb clarity, as though the country is seen through a magnifying glass. As often, humidity banks up like a fine miasma, tinting distance a soft mist blue, and the honeyed afternoon light lies heavily across the air like bars of dusty gold.

Dawn and dusk coax magical reflections from clouds, especially over the gently breathing swell of the Lake. Towering meringues of apricot and peach, shot with lilac mother-of-pearl, or molten rivers of volcano red and tongues of orange fire lie across strata of banked cloud, the shifting mirror of water a deepening echo of the splendour. In the hazy midday, when the mountains of Mozambique or Tanzania melt into misty sky and the edge of water fades away, lake, sky and earth are one seamless continuum, a dreamlike whole. Reality shudders in the heat-haze. Malawi itself seems as ephemeral as reflected light, and how you respond to it reflects yourself.

Malawi seems to provoke a jumble of emotions. The people themselves are both joyous and fearful, and the *wazungu* fortunate enough to live and work there are both dazzled and frustrated. Whatever you expect of Malawi, you will probably be disappointed. But you will also be surprised, and enchanted. Whatever Malawi is, it is not what it seems.

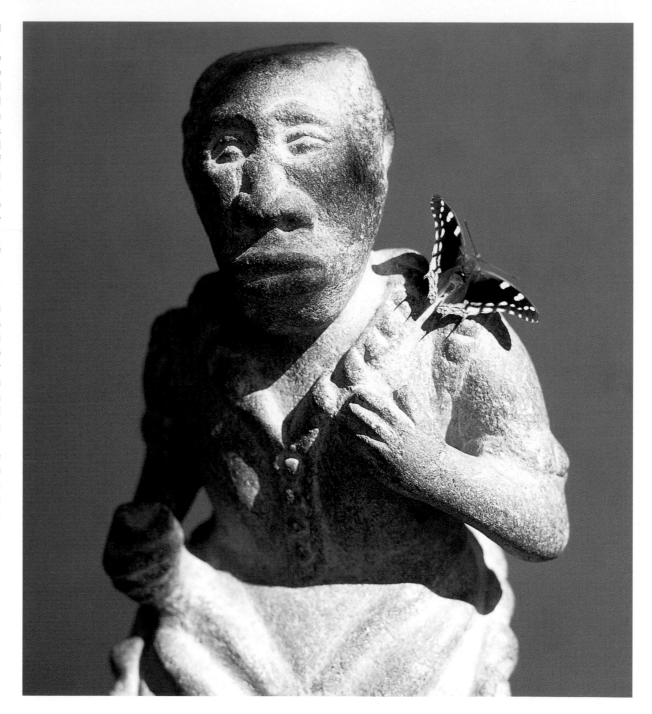

Highlights

Malawi's amazing mountains are a decorous misty blue. They abound, dotted about like a collection of sample mountain designs. If one is short and squat, the next is sharply alpine, another totters dizzily over a plunging ravine, while its neighbour is flat-topped. Yet another is a tumbled heap of boulders. They don't match up neatly, which makes them constantly fascinating. They look like a training ground for apprentice angels in the Divine Design Department.

Opposite, An aerial view of Mulanje with highest peak, Sapitwa, in the distance

Sunrise over the main massif in winter, taken from Thyolo

Chambe rises (above) in an almost sheer rock face of 6000 feet(1800m) feet

Mulanje

The single most remarkable thing about the really high mountains is that they are isolated from the flat plains below. Each is, to some extent, an *inselberg*, a highly individualistic pile thrusting up from a relatively flat area, with a singular collection of vegetation, the dramatic difference in altitude providing a diversity of climatic conditions. Nyika is the northernmost, and the most extensive high plateau in Central Africa. But for sheer height, Mulanje takes the prize.

There is something irresistibly emotional in the human response to mountains. I think it has to do with the inclination of one's head as you crank your chin up to take in sheer size, but the mass of the massif is in direct proportion to the emotional response. Mulanje is the highest peak in central Africa. Mulanje has moved people to tears. Whether your response is one of stomach-crimping awe or heart-racing excitement, the chances are that you will still acknowledge that there is something illusive and mysterious about Mulanje.

Mulanje, clothed in a pale winter light, glowers across the Phalombe plain to Zomba

Sapitwa is clearly visible above the ordered ranks of the tea bushes on Lujeri Estate

Mulanje towers above the surrounding plain - photographed from Thyolo Mountain

For a start there's often the difficulty of simply getting a good look at it. In winter, the mountain hides in smoke-laden air as thick as sea-water, where sunlight filters through in bars. The whole is air-force-blue and almost indistinguishable from the sky. In summer the massif is veiled in moisture, the air milky with mist, and the flanks of Mulanje melt into powder blue above the vivid green carpet of tea. Then there are days when the *chiperoni* sweeps over and the mountain gathers storm clouds around its bulk like a wizard wrapped in a cloak.

Once in a while, Mulanje appears crystal clear, and the mountain is magnificent. Majestic, awe-inspiring and mystical; waterfalls in delicate threads lacing the sheer rock faces; secret green forests in folds and creases; soaring rock mossed over with grasses; groins and screes, chimneys and cols and peaks enough to engage mountaineers for years and years.

On the southern side, neat tea estates are quilted to the base of the mountain, manicured as Japanese gardens, fierce emerald and lime green against the non-committal pastel of the mountain. Wandering swathes of dark green

riverine forest cut through the contour-hugging velvet tea plantations, where cold, sweet streams that danced and leaped from boulder-strewn crevices become strong young rivers. They are overhung with giant forest trees decked with orchids and ferns, a carpet of moss and scarlet lilies between their buttressed trunks; tree ferns grow as big as palm trees, and Mulanje is glimpsed between branches hung with lianas, graced with birds.

Laurens van der Post saw Mulanje as menacing, malicious and sombre, but that was coloured by his experiences on the mountain. It is as extreme as the rest of Africa, and to the unwary it could be thought fickle. People still lose their lives up there, lost in the impenetrable, blinding cold of a sudden *chiperoni*. But many more return unscathed, their eyes

still full of the distant solitude and intimate wonder which Mulanje provides. Of course, there is no easy route up - it's all on foot or not at all, and that too engenders a deeply personal feeling for the mountain. Scattered mountain huts give shelter to the nimble and allow the love affair to last for days. Mulanje is just too vast for a brief flirtation.

More easily accessible to the less robustly adventurous is Zomba Mountain, though here, too, the *chiperoni* comes speeding across the Phalombe plain like a Valkyrie and smothers the plateau in frigid, dripping mist. But, having reached the top by car, the solution is either to retreat to the town below, or hole up in the mountain-top hotel. It's here - in a lovely inn on a mountaintop in tropical Africa - that you'll find blazing log fires on wintry evenings and sometimes even

A weary climber after the ascent to the Lichenya Plateau; in the distance is the well-wooded Chambe Basin

Conical Mount Chiperone in Mozambique is used as a barometer for impending drizzly weather in the Shire Highlands

The view from Ku Chawe, the luxurious mountain-top retreat on Zomba plateau

when it's not so wintry. On summer days, foray forth on horseback, mountain bike or foot to breathe an air, washed so pure and clean by this same beneficent *chiperoni*, that you might wonder about any return to any city...

The name *chiperoni* comes from a mountain perched like a pyramid south-east of Malawi on the plains of Mozambique. From the tea slopes of Thyolo mountain or Mulanje, one can see the weather building around Mount Chiperone, just fifty kilometres or so away. The wind sweeps in, dragging warm moisture-laden air from the Mozambique channel. It hurls itself against the Mulanje massif in swirling clouds of clammy mist, and can turn a beautiful day into a climber's nightmare in minutes. Zomba mountain, some 1000m lower and less than a hundred kilometres behind Mulanje, catches an undiminished blast minutes later.

These cold, wet, misty conditions are what make the Malawi tea industry possible, and water the fabled Mulanje cedars. Most of that condensate of coastal waters would sail past if not intercepted by foliage. It is wetter in the so-called shelter of the trees on Zomba than out in the open during a *chiperoni*.

Groping your way round the Zomba plateau in a chilling fog, it is hard to appreciate the *chiperoni*, but it's evident the mountain does. There is a mist of jacaranda, blue *ageratum* flowers, clouds of pink *dombeya* blossoms, and dew decked spider webs as beaded as belly dancers. Though the golden everlastings close their sunny faces, the yellow daisies are made of sterner stuff, and riot among mauve and purple *vernonia*. In the rains the orchids appear - by the field-full, and in a range of startling reds, pinks and blues. Some, like one beautiful *disa*, are unique enough to the plateau to have earned the specific *zombica*.

Without the *chiperoni*, the wrap-around views are glorious. From the hotel the view out over the plain towards Mulanje is magnificent. Clouds heap up like surf around the low hills, and the town lies beneath them like Atlantis. The powdery sweep of Lake Chilwa, its island a mountain in its own right, is as magical as a place in a fairy tale. Mulanje itself looks long and squat, the layers of mist and smoke drawing subtle stripes across its wide bulk.

From the western side, the ground drops away in sheets of rock and tumbling green forests, and far below, a level

plain half conceals the glinting quicksilver thread of the Shire River. Far, far away, the Kirk Range crumples the horizon. Blue (samango) monkeys chip and chonk in dark trees hung with Spanish moss and epiphytes, and orange *Acrea* butterflies flutter above the heath like animated confetti. A riot of soft summer grass leans gently away from the breeze, and fluffy teased-out clouds shift across the sky.

Malawi has wonderful biotic wealth in these Afro-montane islands like Zomba, Mulanje, Chongoni, Dedza and Nyika. Chief among them is a host of endemic forest birds. Between Zomba Mountain and the town, for instance, there are five species of bulbuls, five different sunbirds, two kinds of twinspots and such unusual charmers as the white-tailed and the wattle-eyed flycatcher, the pygmy kingfisher and the redfaced crimson-wing.

Children from a village on the Lujeri Estate.

Children (below) on Zomba plateau – at Chingwe's Hole - offer rock crystals and bunches of everlasting flowers to the visitor

The spur road to Chingwe's Hole at the very edge of the plateau can be clearly seen in this aerial photograph of Zomba plateau

In the wild

Twenty percent of Malawi is given over to conservation in National Parks, Wildlife and Forest Reserves. That is an impressive proportion, one to which most countries would aspire. However, Malawi is also one of the poorest countries in the world. There is precious little by way of available resources to nurture conservation ideals. Wildlife parks and forestry reserves are generally a little run-down and eroded, and there is not so much wildlife around any more.

But the protected areas are still, surprisingly, well respected by the majority of Malawi's huge population, and some ideas of the area's natural wealth can be gleaned from these areas. There are relics of wonderful forests, sweeping plateaux, glimpses of the lake as it was, the excitement of Malawi's plethora of *inselbergs* and the delight of endemic plants and birds. Malawi is a very beautiful country, and the remarkable natural beauty that so captivated David Livingstone is still to be seen in snatches, in and through these pockets of conservation.

Nyika

The Nyika is the most extensive high plateau in the whole of the Cental African region. Yet once there, it's hard to believe it is Africa. The high and rolling hills, smoothed with grass and coyly forested in the folds, feel like some section of Europe, or a transplanted moorland from England.

From the heights you see no trace of habitation, just undulating grass and wild high sky. Scraped roads snake over the crests of hills. Those, and the relative scarcity of

The dramatic view from Jalawe viewpoint extends across Lake Malawi to the Livingstone Mountains of Tanzania

Bushbuck are commonly seen around the edges of the forest and the rarer aloes such as mzimbana *grow well among sheltered rocks on rocky outcrops*

The beautiful blue orchid
Herschelianthe baurii *is seen*
between September and December
when the surrounding grass is brown

At Chelinda Bridge the river starts its
long descent; there is a series of scenic
waterfalls below the bridge

wildlife, betray the ample presence of man. In winter the hills are patched with an irregular burn pattern: golden and velvety where the grass is untouched; where charred stubble shows the red earth below, the hillside gleams purple like the flank of a hippo, or is ostrich-skin textured with ant-hills. Old burns form a charcoal background to tufts and tussocks of wild-flowers in yellow and purple, pink, scarlet and blue - like a Persian carpet, many say.

In summer the rains turn the carpet to a sea of greens - emerald and jade, sage and olive, even turquoise and silver - and still more flowers delight the eye, red-hot-pokers, gladioli, lilies and orchids, proteas and daisies. The skies, too, have a special splendour. Vast indigo banks of cloud, silver shawls of mist, the snowy opulence of boiling thunderheads.

And always the backdrop of smoothly rolling land, rising and falling like deep breathing, serene and motionless as sleep.

The hills seem treeless. It's always a relief to find them huddled in the hollows, as if escaping from the cold and the wind. And perhaps they need to. The cool air deceives given the fierceness of the sun. But if that is the cost of the spectacular wrap-around views of non-African Africa rolling away on every side it's a minimal one.

There are still plenty of animals. It's the very size of Nyika that spreads their populations thinly over hundreds of square kilometres. Reedbuck many claim to be in inexplicable decline from the thousands which were to be seen in the seventies, while eland and roan antelope, zebra and bushbuck seem to be thriving although, worryingly, most around the Chelinda Forest and the safety of the tourist areas and National Parks offices.

One of the highest parts of the Nyika, close to Nganda Hill, is Jalawe Viewpoint, where the grass is a soft eland-brown, alive and glossy as a pelt. Here the jelly-mould heights plunge to falling ranges rugged as crumpled paper. The ground drops away to distant blue valleys and the far mountain ridges are storm-cloud purple in the smoke-laden air. On the high ridge deep green mountain trees are wind sculpted to Van Gogh silhouettes, and on the sunny slopes yellow-leafed shrubs blaze like a thousand burning bushes.

Centuries-old game trails, a foot or more deep, have cut antique contour paths between them. One thousand metres below the viewpoint it is often possible to count, with binoculars, the elephant which tread those remote meadows and it is from there that occasional marauding lions steal across the plateau.

It is so still up there. Just the sweep of the wind and the grass heads whispering like the ocean. There is an occasional distant view of gliding wings - blackbreasted snake eagle, augur buzzard, circling vultures, and the ragged shapes of white-necked ravens.

On the way down, sixty-eight adult eland and a dozen calves drifted like a dream across the road. Eland are the most subtly elegant of all the antelope. They breathe a timeless enchantment, and to see a herd of eland is to feel especially blessed. They drew the glory of the day after them, and when they had gone, even the grass seemed duller.

The Nyika variety of **Selago thyrsoidea** *forms a small shrub and attracts instant attention in the dry grassland*

Porcupine quills are found on all the roads on the Nyika but the animal itself is more rarely seen

The view from Domwe viewpoint looking north and west

Opposite; looking down to Chelinda Bridge and River from Chelinda Hill

A roan antelope takes fright at Lake Kaulime where they are commonly found feeding on water-weed

Fingira Rock, right, has paintings in a cave half way to the summit

The lovely Mbuzizinandi road offers spectacular views over the escarpment especially in the evening light

There are roan antelope too, but roan do not seem real. Roan are the invention of Hollywood, Disney donkeys done up posh and made to stand like show-dogs with tassels on their ears and their hind quarters lower than their shoulders. Such a jumble of bits; those huge silly ears, a donkey's mane and a cow's tail. Their faces are an approximation of an African mask by someone who has never been to Africa, big white patches around the eyes and the nose - crude and unimaginative. It makes the poor things look like stuffed toys, each with a neatly stitched Y-shaped nose. Roan look like they are designed for the under twelve movie-going mob, not to survive the rigours of this hungry continent.

The road back through rolling hills and acid green bracken fields to Chilinda pine plantation, perched on the brow of a hill like a corduroy patch on a silk coverlet. Against a brooding curtain of old pines the new Lodge looks like a misplaced bit of Bavaria around a stone replica of a moon-rocket. The architecture has been variously described as inspired, bizarre, imaginative... Whatever it claims to be it's certainly a most comfortable place. The stone rocket is alleged to be a tribute to the fabled Nyika honey, immortalised by Laurens van der Post in his best selling *Venture to the Interior* written in the mid-twentieth century just prior to the planting of the extensive pine plantations at Chilinda

It's a strange place, the Nyika, this Europe-flavoured Africa with its unreal antelope and its most unusual lodge - but you'll find that Nyika draws you back. There is too much, and too little, there for you to be free of it.

*Accommodation at Chelinda ranges
from the luxurious, at the quaintly
designed Lodge, left, with its views
across the central grasslands to Dam 3,
through the original rustic chalets by
Dam One (above) to simple tented
camp facilities*

*Guests enjoy close-range game viewing
from horseback, also offered by the
Nyika Safari Company*

*Nyika National Park is the largest of Malawi's
parks, nearly 3200 square kilometres.
It covers the entire Malawian part of the Nyika
plateau, and adjoins the Zambian border to the west.*

*The vegetation is short montane grassland.
Dambos and evergreen forest patches are found on
the plateau heights; Brachystegia woodland, protea
and heath scrub on the lower slopes. The wildflowers
are a particular attraction; Nyika is regarded as the
richest orchid area in south-central Africa, with over
200 species of orchids already recorded.*

*This is not "big five" country. It's sad that modern
tourists seem to think they deserve to see all of
Africa's treasures in a day, as if life is some kind of
fast-food outlet. Hours of patient watchfulness bring
such a great reward to those who value what they
see. Apart from the animals already mentioned,
kudu, buffalo, samango or blue monkey, baboon
and leopard are periodically sighted; jackal, spotted
hyena and warthog are prevalent.*

*The Nyika begs to be explored on foot, and the
absence of major predators in large numbers makes
this possible. Ardent birders, botanists and hikers
will revel in the diversity and space. There are intimate
horseback safaris for the more athletic, and that's a
wonderful way of coming to terms with this distant,
non-committal landscape, as well as getting really
close to the animals.*

*The lodge and chalets are on the fringe of the
pine plantation at Chelinda, and roughly 2300
metres above sea level. It is cool even at the
height of summer, when misty rain can set in
for several days. It's always cold at night.*

Elephant are again commonly seen in Vwaza Marsh by the shores of Lake Kazuni close to the Safari Camp. Hippo have always been long term residents.

Walking safaris are encouraged but an armed guard is essential

Vwaza Marsh Game Reserve

At the height of the dry season, Vwaza is a landscape drawn in pastels, grey and fawn and Naples yellow on the textured paper of a smoke-hazed sky. The central African plateau is enlivened with hills, each outlined in a scaffolding of leafless flat-topped trees, like delicate cobwebs. These are *brachystegia glaucescens*, the beautiful misnamed mountain-acacia. Their graceful limbs become rich with the spring flush, tinting the hills copper and bronze and royal crimson.

The shortcut from the Nyika Plateau down to Vwaza cuts through Katumbi, and it's one of the loveliest routes to travel. The road is an unimproved track through a host of tobacco and maize planted smallholdings. Plumes of dust, fine as cake-flour and red as rust, trail behind each vehicle and bronze the leaves on either side of the track. Small neat villages straggle along between the hills and the roadside, and tall *Acacia albidas* shade patchwork fields.

The entrance to the Reserve teeters on the lip of a settlement, goats skip and skitter across the road, and chickens scatter. To the left an old metal bridge crosses the South Rukuru River and a road runs along the southern limit of the park, accompanied by a scattering of houses. Just inside the park fence the South Rukuru spreads over a small flood plain and forms Lake Kazuni which shrinks to dry mud-bed and expands again with the rains to a truly respectable lake. A small group of four reeded "chalets", run by the Nyika Safari Company, are to the left, between the road and the high-water line of the Lake.

David Foot

But do not be misled - for all its unprepossessing setting, Vwaza is capable of considerable magic. More animals can be seen around Lake Kazuni than in many other of Malawi's parks, and if one hears the crowing of roosters along with the wild African dawn chorus - well, why not? Mankind has been part of the African landscape from time immemorial.

Travelling north into the body of the park itself doesn't alter the awareness of human presence, though the park was never more than lightly populated.

Vwaza has the northernmost occurrence, in all of Africa, of *mopane* trees, their rough fissured trunks tall and dark against the pale earth. Mostly, though, it's *miombo* woodland, and distant views show a world coloured grey and beige, russet and purple, cream and sage under the smoky jacaranda blue of the sky.

The northern limit of the park is the fabled Vwaza Marsh - once one of the most ivory-rich areas of Africa, a famous hunting ground in the days of ivory and slaves - a huge open savanna plain among the endless *masasa* trees. This vast *dambo* shimmers with waving grasses and ground orchids in summer, but in the closing months of the winter dryness the area is a rolling vista of crusted black-cotton soil, pockmarked with the dried imprint of hundreds of hoofed feet, and bristly with the charred stubble of burned stalks.

Before the distant rim of hills a few scorched palm trees sag against the heat-haze, and a dust-devil toss scraps of grass into the milky sky. Nothing else moves, no squirrels, no duiker, no baboons. A single martial eagle turns slowly on the axis of the air and emphasises the emptiness.

With the absence of water, and nothing left but the driest and least palatable of the grasses, the game has moved off - at least so it would seem, since the dry earth shows they were there when the ground was wet. So hopefully they will be back with the rain, and won't have been eaten across the western boundary in Zambia, or north, east and south in Malawian villages. The bulk of the wildlife may have gone into the pot in years past; yet to judge from the small but growing populations around Lake Kazuni, with care and protection and time, it will all come back again.

Rob House

With a measure of control achieved over local poaching activity at Vwaza, the elephant have returned to the sanctuary and their numbers are growing

A buffalo herd by the shores of Lake Kazuni

Elephants

More than a century ago, Vwaza Marsh was renowned through East Africa for its ivory, and there is no record of how many elephants were killed then, but the numbers must have been considerable. Remarkably, elephants are again Vwaza's great attraction, now they have returned after an uneasy absence of two years.

Relic populations maintain a toe-hold in the south-east corner of Vwaza, clustering around the permanent water provided by Lake Kazuni and protected by the proximity of a tourist camp and the Parks and Wildlife Offices.

At the New Lodge is a dining room, an open space under thatch which serves as lounge, bar and dining area, which provides a wonderful, uninterrupted view of Lake Kazuni. It also provides as electrifying an experience of the Vwaza elephants as you are ever likely to have.

Sit there contentedly after dinner, the paraffin lamps extinguished, wait for moonrise to light the lake and illuminate the gentle pageant of kudu and impala, and perhaps even buffalo coming to the hippo-heaving water to drink. Then with evening's soft breath, listen to the distant crunch and pop of elephant, just visible in the moonlight, feeding in the reeds, and the occasional trumpeted squeal of irritation from an adult or derision from a juvenile. The creamy cloud of the Milky Way glows between the dark lacework of thorn tree

David Foot

David Foot

Just under a thousand square kilometres in size, Vwaza Marsh Wildlife has miles and miles of featureless Brachystegia woodland which many find dull and monotonous. The greater area of Vwaza Wildlife Reserve can seem (in the late dry season) empty of game.

But Vwaza has one of the most well judged wildlife lodges in Malawi, offering minimalist accommodation laced with the luxury of private bathrooms and hot water. A cook is available to spare slaving over an open fire, and a fully catered service is available. You can sit on your tiny private verandah and sip a cold beer while watching the hippos in Lake Kazuni, or the buffalo ambling past. There is little reason to wander far from Lake Kazuni

Around Lake Kazuni there are tall trees, acacia, and more wooden-pear (Shrebera trichloclada) leafless and laden with innumerable tiny little pears, like early Christmas decorations. The woody pod splits in two and opens like a miniature hippo's mouth to release the winged seeds, but stays on the tree for ages afterwards.

Near the lake tsetse flies don't occur, so take advantage of the even terrain to do a bit of walking. Visitors must be accompanied by a National Parks guide.

The birding is wonderful. Forked tailed drongo, emeruld spotted wood dove, puff-backed shrike, tropical boubou, pale billed hornbill and Cape batis are commonly, or uncommonly, seen. Meyers parrots shriek cheekily among the acacia seed pods. Further into the park martial eagle, black eagle, brown snake eagle and bateleur patrol the skies. The Vwaza "special" is the rare white winged starling, which is only found in the Rumphi district adjoining Zambia.

branches and the elephant-scent of rich mown grass provides an unforgettable memory as they arrive. Moving silently out of the reeds, each seems a gathering darkness, like a shadow solidified, a condensation of ghostly grey moonlight.

They drift up the close-cropped grass, drawn by the amber spicy lure of thorn-tree pods. Gradually the entire group draws closer. The trees around the dining room are *acacia* and marula and when the *acacia* pods are over, the marula fruit is ripe, beloved of the elephants and drawing them from great distances.

Kasungu

Smack in the middle of Malawi are the twin reserves of Kasungu and Nkhotakota, the first hugging the border with Zambia, the second close to the lakeside. They are often spoken of in one breath, as if they are one unit. In fact they are about 100 kilometres apart and are vastly different.

Where Kasungu National Park is on the flat central African plateau and is a jigsaw of *dambos* and often scrubby *brachystegia* woodland, Nkhotakota Wildlife Reserve is on the escarpment, wild hilly country with the odd high patch of ancient, thick montane forest.

Kasungu, at first glance, could be called uninspiring — the vistas of *brachystegia*, despite the grace of the trees themselves and their spectacular spring colouring, can appear monotonous. This is the sort of landscape that would invoke a stifled yawn from dedicated townies, and even the bush-baptised can find it a little irritating.

Also *brachystegia* woodland is notoriously bad game viewing country. There is just too much cover, and those animals that enjoy the woodlands know how to use them to best

The ground hornbill is becoming less common throughout Malawi

Lifupa Lodge in the centre of Kasungu National Park offers a comfortable base for a memorable environmental experience. The dam with its resident hippos contains high fish populations and angling is encouraged

effect, and are very hard to see. Nevertheless, the woodland often gives way to grassy *dambos*, meadow areas of marshy grassland, and these are wonderful spotting grounds.

Here you'll see oribi, a little gazelle-like antelope, a reddish-gold ram-rod upright creature with a distinctive black tufted tail. Curiosity not only killed the cat, but it has done the oribi a severe disservice too. Their inquisitiveness has made them an easy target for hunters, so it's quite a thrill to see one.

There may be a tubby little Sharpe's grysbok, even smaller than the oribi, barrelling away through the grass like an

*O*ver 2300 square kilometres in extent, almost
half of the western boundary of Kasungu
National Park lies along the border with Zambia.
The scenery is flat and undulating with a few
isolated granite outcrops or inselbergs. The
vegetation is predominantly brachystegia, grassy
dambos with Fourea and protea Gaguedi.
There are open woodlands of terminalia, acacia
and combretum along major drainage lines.
Over 300 bird species have been recorded. There are
ancient iron smelting kilns in the more remote parts.
A cluster of old-fashioned but very comfortable
rondavels comprise the only tourist accommodation
and an excellent restaurant supports the Park's claim
to domestic and international tourism.

overgrown rabbit, its fat brown haunches bunched and
bobbing - a truly Jack Russell sized antelope.

Reedbuck stand statue-still against the fringe of forest
around the *dambo*. Medium-sized and graceful, its corrugated
horns form gentle crescents above the alert head, rather like
a miniature waterbuck.

It is as well that leopard and lion are occasionally seen, for
the scarcity of game in Kasungu is now very noticeable.
Less than twenty years ago, Kasungu was Malawi's premier
Park. It boasted the largest population of elephant in Malawi,
not to mention lion, cheetah, wild dog, and black rhino.
Today the beautifully sited and well-appointed Lifupa Lodge
must emphasise all the other attractions of the Park such as
the splendid fishing in the dam right in front. Here hippo are
certain to be seen wallowing in the shallows, to the delight of
visitors at the Lodge.

Nkhotakota

Nkhotakota Wildlife Reserve sprawls headlong down the western escarpment of the Rift Valley, tumbling almost to the edge of Lake Malawi itself. Threading through its woodlands and evergreen forests are a tumble of streams and rivulets, and two main rivers. The Dwangwa marks the northernmost limit of the Reserve, the Bua River almost cuts the Reserve in two.

The Bua is possibly Malawi's longest river. It rises in the Mchinji area near Mozambique in the west and travels north-east across the broadest part of the country before slicing through the peaked and pleated woodlands of Nkhotakota on its final rush to the lake.

For a river that has trekked across the broadest part of this densely populated country, and then wriggled and squirmed its way down the escarpment of the Great Rift, it is neither exhausted by its travels nor overburdened with silt.

With a hiss like a giant blow torch, the Bua shimmies and glitters. Shapes of fish thread its depth and young fry stitch spangles in its shallows. Pied kingfishers hang like six-winged cherubim above the smoother reaches. Green-backed herons skulk among the reeds and rocks. From overhanging branches giant kingfishers, opulent in charcoal and russet and silver, pontificate in voices thin as party-squeakers. Trumpeter hornbills wail like disappointed children, and crowned hornbills flap past quacking like rubber toys.

A flash of black and white from an *Acacia albida* across the river draws the eye. Here at Bua Camp the river is as wide as a soccer pitch, and the opposite bank rises from a rocky edge to a steep tree-clad hill. Too far to see well, binoculars help identify the splash of white as the breast of a palmnut vulture.

This is the smallest of the vultures, rare in the south but

Njobvu Safari Lodge is on a beautiful white sand beach and is the closest accommodation for a visit to Nkhotakota Game Reserve

The pied kingfisher is commonly seen throughout Malawi

The Bua River flows through the Reserve and limited, licensed, fishing is available for, among other species, the lake salmon or mpasa

fairly common in the rest of Africa, occurring wherever oil palms or raffia palms grow. The tree itself seems to be hung with what could be hamerkop nests, if there were less of them. This is an indigenous species of "elephant's ear" fern, *Platycerium elephantotois*, some almost a metre high from top to bottom! These giant ferns form the hanging gardens of Bua.

The base of dried leaves thrusts up above the supporting branch like a crown. In places these have weathered away to a lacy fretwork of veins like a skeletal tiara above the plant. Pockets of detritus are trapped behind them, a fertile patch for tree-gardens. A thriving community of plants flourish - grasses, weeds, orchids and more ferns. Mosses grow beneath the giant ferns, and other ferns and orchids thread their roots among the interlaced bases. Aerial roots hang down, and seed-heads peep from above the parapet of dried fronds. Here and there the growing central leaf of the giant fern curls from the domed boss like a pleated green tongue; more often it is split into two, like twin whirls of wind from a cherub's face on an antique map.

Nkhotakota is indeed beautiful. But it takes some dedication to see it. Access is unmarked and needs a four-wheel drive vehicle even in the dry season. There are few roads in the Reserve itself, and no accommodation within the park. The nearest, to international standards, is the Njobvu Safari Lodge on a beautiful part of the Lakeshore south of Nkhotakota. Wildlife is relatively abundant and the Reserve has probably the only breeding lion population in the country. There are reports of buffalo and roan and many sightings of elephant at night and along the rivers.

The Nkhotakota Reserve is a little under 2000 square kilometres of steep, hilly terrain of mainly Brachystegia *woodland. Chipata Mountain has evergreen forest on its slopes.*

The Chipata Mountain camping site and wilderness school burned down several years ago and has not been rebuilt. There is a designated camping site on the Bua River below the Reserve's scout camp, but there are no facilities to speak of. Water is available from the river - mind the crocs and boil it first. For the rest, you must take everything you need.

The Bua River is one of the most important breeding sites for the lake salmon, or mpasa, *a good sporting fish. Some angling is allowed, check with the Department of Fisheries for permits and regulations.*

Parks and People

Lake Malawi National Park

The extraordinary thing about this World Heritage Site and the foremost of Malawi's National Parks is that nobody knows about it. Everyone knows about Cape Maclear, and lots of people recognise the name Monkey Bay. But Lake Malawi National Park? Never heard of it.

Does this make it a candidate for the "best kept secret" tag - in a country which once used that national description in its efforts to create more tourism interest? No, not really. The word "secret" implies that somebody would want to know but the overwhelming ethos at Lake Malawi National Park seems to be "nobody cares".

The fall of Malawi's topmost tourist attraction is a case of the ill wind. Back in the old days when South Africa was political anathema to the rest of the world, there was only one country in Africa ready to welcome these pariah tourists. Malawi. South Africans visited in droves, since there was really nowhere else for them to go, at least north of the Limpopo. Malawi, especially the Southern Lakeshore resorts and Cape Maclear, were favourite honeymoon and holiday destinations throughout the 70's and 80's.

The winds of change arrived even in South Africa, and South Africans are now welcome everywhere in Africa. But Golden Sands, the resort area within Lake Malawi National Park, has tourist figures a fraction of what they were in the early 90's, before isolated South Africa became the New Rainbow Nation and had a bewildering array of novel African options.

The bustle of the crowded Chembe beach at dawn contrasts with the peaceful serenity of the Cape Maclear area and its adjacent islands

*The dugout fishermen are still
there but more often now it
is tourism which provides
their main income - from
those who visit for diving,
kayaking, sailing and other
'eco-pursuits'*

Looking at Golden Sands today, one can see that it must once have been heart-catchingly beautiful. The shattered terraces spill broken bricks down bald slopes; shards of concrete and rusting tins congregate in hollows, scattered with the fallen blossoms of flame trees and frangipani. The "luxury" bungalows have torn mosquito netting, limp curtains and sagging mattresses. Buckled paving catches at unwary feet.

All of this overlooks a biscuit-coloured beach and the sparkling turquoise and teal of the crystal cool lake. Fragrant green flowers from the pod mahogany tree *(Afzelia quanzensis)* lay their waxy cheeks on the sand, and a thousand tiny fishes in the glassy shallows rush up to examine your toes. Across the water, forested and rocky islands look like heaped mohair blankets on biscuit bases, and the air is full of cormorants, kingfishers, fish eagles, wagtails, hamerkops and more.

*L*ake Malawi National Park is an internationally proclaimed World Heritage Site, and was the first such park in the world declared to protect tropical freshwater fish. It is an intensely beautiful area of vitally important bio-diversity.

There are over 600 known species of the colourful lake cichlids so popular with the aquarium trade. However, swimming within the curve of the main Cape Maclear beach should be avoided due to bilharzia, which is acknowledged to be a real threat. Snorkelling and diving around the islands further out is considered quite safe.

A luxurious big catamaran with the very latest equipment can be chartered from Danforth Yachting at Cape Maclear, and Kayak Africa runs two superb eco-friendly camps on Domwe and Mumbo Islands out of their base deep within Chembe Village.

Accommodation within the National Park consists at the time of writing of six very basic rondavels. However, a progressive National Parks development policy seeks development of the old Golden Sands site from the private sector. With active and sympathetic management Lake Malawi National Park could reassert itself as the prime tourism resort on the Southern Lakeshore.

Kayak Africa runs two comfortable eco-lodges on Domwe (right) and Mumbo (opposite and above) Islands

In the heart of Lake Malawi National Park (the first freshwater conservation area in Africa) is Cape Maclear. It's a four kilometre crescent of golden beach running from Otter Point to Chembe Lodge, and right in the middle of that is the enclave village of Chembe.

How do you run a National Park when smack in the middle of it is an area that is not classified as Park, and is home to an unknown number of people? Conservative estimates say four thousand souls. There are other estimates of five and seven thousand, and growing fast. Every villager is supported by fishing and tourism, and the dusty expanse of hand hoed fields between the village and the wooded foothills show the need for proper cultivation. The thin exhausted soil washes down to the water's edge where new reed beds demonstrate the start of a rapidly expanding delta.

Mud-and-thatch houses with reed enclosed yards form a belt some ten to twelve houses deep along the line of the beach. It's an organic, erratic area of dwellings and fish-drying racks, tiny restaurants and the occasional tourist lodge, like Steven's, Fat Monkey's, Chembe Lodge and several others.

The broad sweep of the Golden Sands site at Cape Maclear may once again become pivotal to tourism development on the southern Lakeshore

There is a raffish charm and hauntingly picturesque quality to Chembe Village. If you like walking, want to get to know the good-natured locals, don't mind dust and can happily do without any luxuries, Cape Maclear's Chembe Village is the place to be. Backpackers love it and most visitors seem to be under 25 years old. Boating and snorkelling are popular, yet the fact that this area boasts the only under-water, self-guided trail anywhere in Africa is unknown. Few know too that Kayak Africa runs a pair of very comfortable and attractive eco-lodges on Domwe and Mumbo islands – one is actually off Mumbo Island - on the tiny Jumbo island adjunct.

Since access to the village does not actually pass through an official gate, it's doubtful if many visitors even know they are surrounded by a National Park.

Opposite: large groups of Liwonde's elephant often visit the Shire River and even swim across it

Lillian's lovebird, a member of the parrot family, is a rare resident in Liwonde while hippo are far from rare - in the protected shelter of a receptive riverine environment

Liwonde National Park

If you look at a map of Malawi you will see Lake Malawi slither down the eastern edge of the country looking very much like a legless sea-beast with jaws agape. Dangling from the tip of its nose by a thread is bite-sized Lake Malombe. The thread happens to be the Shire River, the single watercourse that drains the second deepest of Africa's great lakes.

Just south of where it leaves Lake Malombe, the Shire slices through the very western edge of Liwonde National Park, which stretches almost to the little town of Liwonde. The broad, swift and silent waters, raucous with the honking of hippos, form a focus of attention. But the Park has a number of specialities apart from the river that make it noteworthy, like Lillian's lovebird, Dickenson's kestrel and the rare red-flowered euphorbia *(Euphorbia lividiflora)*.

The lovebirds are little feathered gems that flash by like green enamelled bullets. You'll hear the unmistakable lovebird shriek, and a small group will screech past, giving just enough of a glimpse to show they are lovebirds of the parrot family, before they vanish into the elegant gallery of *mopane* trees.

Liwonde National Park is more than noteworthy in anyone's book. It's frankly beautiful, reminiscent of Mozambique's Gorongoza on a small scale, with lush flood plains and festive palms. The three hills that give this flat area definition are speckled with evenly strewn black rocks and lightly wooded *miombo* with *combretum*, *commiferae* and the softly gleaming,

ghostly trunk of the occasional large leafed star chestnut *(Sterculia quinqueloba)*.

Like all of Malawi's parks, Liwonde has suffered terribly from the demands of poverty. Poaching for the pot, as well as really devastating commercial poaching, can happen under the noses of any under-staffed, under-funded administration. This is not to say that there is no game in Liwonde - compared to Gorongoza today, the park is fairly rampant with wildlife. Elephant and hippo are plentiful. The Park has the only black rhino in Malawi. There are also sable, waterbuck, impala, bushbuck and kudu though not all in the sort of numbers one might expect in the 538 square kilometres that make up the Park.

Currently Malawi's premier wildlife destination, Liwonde National Park is 538 square kilometres of fertile flood plain, lowland evergreen thicket, fever-tree forests, and tall mopane *woodland hung with python vines and starred with impala lilies.*

The broad Shire River runs the length of the western side of the park. In the wet, the only access to the northern part is by boat. Perched on a bank of the river is a privately run tourist facility, Mvuu Wilderness Camp and Lodge. The name was an obvious choice, for in Chichewa mvuu *is the name for hippo, and the Shire River is alive with them. There are also many crocodiles and a wonderful array of water-birds.*

Liwonde National Park boasts a count of 410 bird species - about two thirds of the total checklist for the whole of Malawi - and several of them are "specials". You can be almost sure of sighting Pels fishing owl - if you ask the guide and are prepared to walk a little.

Liwonde has greater numbers and a wider diversity of animals than any other Malawi park. Two or three lions, thought to have come back down from Mozambique, have returned after a mysterious absence of several years. Since they can be extremely aggressive, walking into the bush on your own is not only forbidden but very foolish.

Within the park is an extensive Rhino Sanctuary, a breeding enclosure sponsored primarily by the J&B Circle within the J&B Care for the Rare programme. This was developed as a high-security enclosure for imported black rhino, and gradually other wildlife species were brought in. The rhinos are breeding well but until the outer perimeter of Liwonde is proven secure, it is unlikely that they will be released from the enclosure.

One of the attractive results of the relative scarcity of game is that the fleshy shrub called *Adenium obesum*, the Sabi star or impala lily, does not get browsed down to a stub as it does further south. In Liwonde the plants grow up to two metres tall and from June to August are a mass of blooms. Rather like miniature baobabs, they are obese indeed. The star-shaped flowers appear on the podgy grey stems like a minor miracle, white or pink with a crinkley crimson border, and in such profusion that the display seems touchingly extravagant, like the flowers at a big funeral.

Game viewing from the rippling silk expanse of the River Shire provides a truly memorable sight. A frieze of dozens of elephants below borassus palms and fever trees, smoke grey backs like an undulating range of hills above an emerald wall of water grass; a splash of white as egrets settle on grey backs; dark green of riverine forest rising beyond, and the pale lilac blue of the distant rift escarpment – this is the epitome of romantic Africa.

The waterside viewing from the tented safari style rooms at the Mvuu Wilderness Lodge is excellent

The beautiful impala lily, with its pink flowers on the ends of bare stems, thrives in Liwonde

Rob House

The long line of animals comes to a halt, and a background noise, a noise like breakers on a beach, the roar of a restless ocean, fades away. Only when it is gone is it obvious what it had been - the sound of hundreds of huge feet splashing knee deep through hidden water.

Then the grey backs are still, like a row of sombre marquees. From among them rise slow deliberate trunks, blind periscopes scanning the breeze for a hint of hostile intention. There is a silent stalemate for long suspended seconds.

Then the group begins to move again, heading without hesitation to a reach of open water. Ears forward at full stretch, trunks and tails raised, the whole crossing is effected with nervous efficiency. Mature animals emerge on the other side glistening wet from the shoulder down, playful

youngsters with a plimsoll line just below the eyes, and the toddling calves, carefully shepherded in the middle of the family, are wet all over. Some pause to frolic in the shallows, while a baby is towed across, trunk clutching mother's tail. Awe comes easy at the sight of such grey grace and gentle power, such single family thought in such a crowd, such huge cohesive action, majestic and serene, the vast panorama of it dominating, that details like a hitch-hiking baby can be missed.

Often it's these close particulars that add texture to the bush experience in Liwonde – a seed you have not seen before, an exceptionally pretty moth, a glimpse of the shy but garrulous thrush-nightingale, or the bloodless violence of Böhm's bee-eaters, battering the wings off moths almost as big as themselves to make a manageable mouthful.

Even gazing at the bare ground is exciting. A smooth sandy place lets you enjoy the scribblings left by the feet of a myriad passing denizens: the tiny little y-shaped prints of blue waxbills, the delicate divided heart shape of impala hooves, the huge dog-like paw mark of a hyaena. An ephemeral and artistic visitor's book.

Mvuu Wilderness Lodge and Camp; a view from the lagoon of the Lodge restaurant and, below, the central complex for the main Camp

The Lower Shire Parks

Dropping from Blantyre to the Shire River through bands of winter smoke and summer haze, the very scenic road snakes down through eucalyptus plantations, bamboo thickets and scattered villages to level out on the broad Shire flood plain. The river itself lies along the reed beds and sandbanks like a huge deep green python, its muscular strength masked by deceptive lethargy.

The road crosses the river at Chikwawa and bowls straight as an arrow through kilometres of towering sugar cane. Areas of indigenous forest remain - Lengwe National Park, the Wildlife Reserves of Majete and Mwabvi, and the sugar estate's own Nyala Park, but around Nchalo, the billiard-table of cane stretches into the hazy distance, bounded by the blue escarpment.

Among the cane fields baobabs lift podgy arms to the sky. It may just have been more economical to leave the arboreal monoliths there than to root them out, but whatever the reason, everyone's grateful. The trees give scale and interest to the monotony of the cane, and somehow link the distant hills to the here and now.

The broad sweep of the Shire valley cradles the heat, and though only one of the parks abuts the river, you are never far from the thought of it. The very humidity of the air carries the river in it.

Majete

The Shire River is an impressive stretch of water. It is the only out-flow in the huge expanse of Lake Malawi. It forms a brief neck between the Lake and the basin of Lake Malombe,

and then spills out again and sweeps strongly along the west side of Liwonde National Park and winds its way down through the falling ground of the Shire Highlands, along the edge of Majete Wildlife Reserve and through the stepped and gushing cataracts of Kapichira Falls to the serene and lush lower Shire Valley.

Kapichira Falls. This was the final blow to Livingstone's vision of a waterborne route as "God's Highway" into Central Africa. Unfortunately visitors can no longer see the cataracts as Livingstone saw them. Spread across the lip of the falls is now the massive wall of a dam, part of Malawi's ambitious hydro-electric scheme.

On the view point, a virtually unspoilt little knoll set with tall trees and rich aloe clumps among the rocks, the visitor gazes up at the broad rococo spills of coffee-coloured water. Rising above them now is a bank of gravel, like the business-like waste dump of a mine. Set in the centre of this are five very impressive concrete flood-gates. It all looks utterly impervious, yet the river still rushes past, as if the dam is an illusion. The juxtaposition of seemingly pristine wilderness and state-of-the-art technology suggests a science-fiction movie set.

Once the first shock passes and the sometimes painful cost of progress is accepted, it's obvious that considerable care has been taken with the dam. There is evidence of thought and some sensitivity in the placing of the turbines, and the unavoidable march of pylons has been screened as much as possible.

A few of these pylons can be seen from the little tourist camp outside the park, but not enough to ruin the spectacular setting. Privately run, and somewhat down-at-heel, the Majete Safari Camp overlooks a turbulent bend in the Shire River below the falls, and across into the adjacent Forest Reserve on the opposite bank. On a small outcrop stands a tiny rock-built thatched chapel, long disused. Built in memory of the missionaries buried nearby - some of the less hardy to follow in Livingstone's fabled footsteps - it now stores fire-wood garnered from the bush and is blackened with wood smoke. But the space is still serene, and the view of the river, framed by a simple stone gothic arch, is deeply moving.

The entrance to Majete Wildlife Reserve is just to the west of the dam, and the park boundary begins above the Safari Camp and runs along the river for about 15 kilometres before swinging west and south again to form a rough circle of hilly

Rob House

*Protection of a dwindling nyala
population - at the northernmost
limit of their range - was the main
reason for the establishment of
Lengwe National Park.
It supports its wildlife through
the provision of boreholes
supplying piped water to
the traditional waterholes*

terrain. It's around 780 square kilometres of park-like *miombo* woodland, with thick riverine bush along the water courses.

Majete too has an air of romantic tragedy about it. It suffers from the same ailment as the other wildlife areas in Malawi; the national economy. There is not enough to pay the scouts, to install or maintain fences and buildings and roads. The roads become impassable in the wet, and the thin stream of tourists dries up. The single existing "chalet" has fallen into disrepair and been taken over as scout accommodation. In 1983 there were elephant, sable, waterbuck, samango money, zebra and buffalo, and many others. There were both whitebacked and lappet faced vultures. There are no elephant now and other species are seldom seen. Majete is the only place in Malawi where one can see rock pratincoles. They nest on islands of rock above the Kapichira Falls, one of the very few nesting sites in southern Africa. The dam submerged some of these rock shelves but still a dozen or so pairs nest here.

Majete is spectacularly beautiful and varied in its scenery and wilderness. There are even hot springs in the western hills, but the roads to them have vanished under several seasons of grass.

Lengwe

There was a time when Lengwe National Park was Malawi's pride and joy. The most popular of the parks, and the best equipped, its boast was a thriving population of nyala, at the northern-most limit of their range.

The nyala are still there, though their numbers are somewhat reduced. The nyala is a tall antelope, its stately air made marginally less impressive by the feeling that you are actually looking at a small kudu in fancy dress.

Nyala looks to be the same overall stature, but is less than half the heft, and where kudu horns loop through expansive outward spirals, the nyala's has a more demure twist. But that's where the restraint stops. Kudu wears a sober pinstripe suit in grey or fawn; nyala goes for charcoal or chocolate. Nyala has puffed out his thigh muscles with feathering and spangled them with bush-buck beauty-spots. He has hung his belly and dewlap with a fringe. He has accentuated the stripes on his back, and as a final flourish, he has pulled on yellow rugby socks. Despite the outfit the wearer contrives great dignity in his wanderings through the thickets that give Lengwe its name.

Despite all that, they are not easy to see. They feel happiest in the security of the thickets, which ironically may have contributed to their fall in numbers. The thicket that gives privacy to nyala gives equal cover to poachers. Game paths through thicket are easy to spot, and useful places to set snares and gin-traps. The years of drought and the mismanagement of the water holes that support the nyala population further contributed to the numbers decline but the park authorities reckon that with new boreholes and piped water supply nyala numbers should go up again.

The arrogant sun-loving buffalo out in the grasslands thrive and prosper. Buffalo are poached too, but not as easily as nyala. And Lengwe National Park maintains the largest herd of buffalo in Malawi. A languid group of three hundred or more, with heavy bosses like molten wax and soapy noses, can often be seen. They wear their horns like 1920's cloche hats, and peer out from under them like a sullen group of overweight flappers. Nothing is as deadly, the hunters remind us, as a wounded buffalo...

The beautiful sable antelope, sophisticated cousin of the comic roan, is thought to inhabit Mwabvi but is now rarely seen

Aside from buffalo and nyala, and graceful ranks of impala like a delicate *corps de ballet*, Lengwe is an extraordinary park. The park encloses some 800 square kilometres of superb Lower Shire Valley vistas. Sweeping parkland of tall grass and taller knob-thorns *(Acacia nigrescens)*, thickets of flame acacia *(A. ataxacantha)* and jesse bush *(Combretum celastroides)* enlivened by tall *miombo* forest patches, and wonderful secretive pools tinted green with duckweed and splashed with blue water lilies. In this jungly tangle are groups of samango monkeys, their elegant dark legs and extra long tails like exclamation points in the bush.

Lengwe is easily one of the loveliest parks in this part of Africa but it is in a state of disrepair. The tourist facilities had attained near derelict status so privatisation looks likely. Many visitors are happy to camp. The roads have been completely rehabilitated but, late in the rainy season, parts may become impassable as they vanish into shoulder-high guinea grass. Progression through it can be preceded by a mini-tsunami of biomass - a wave of grass seeds, grasshoppers, stick insects, bugs and beetles, moths and mantises, caterpillars and stink-bugs, butterflies, ants and weevils - a wonderland of winged and wingless species.

Mwabvi Wildlife Reserve

It's less than three hours to Mwabvi from Blantyre. The most southern of Malawi's protected areas and the smallest of the Reserves, it is a little gem. Some areas are naturally imbued with an additional sense of grace, and Mwabvi has it. As the dusty track dips to cross the threshold stream, there are glimpses of elegant forest.

Entering the park is rather like opening the door on a long forgotten attic or basement. The place is a wonderland of little relic habitats, fragments of a Shire Valley that no longer exists, small remnants of vegetation types set in exquisite frames of varied landscapes. Initially proclaimed to protect the last few black rhino in the area, the park has lost more than a third of its land, and certainly all of its rhino.

Between rising ledges of rock lies a wonderland of cool kranzes and glassy green pools. Rock fig and tall *brachystegia* dapple the sandstone, and the river *dombeyea* leans gently down to scatter creamy petals on ledges graced with fading fern and tenacious aloes. An undulating woodland canopy is framed by leafy, creeper hung branches and underscored by the warm gold of rock plunging down to the last thread of the summer's stream.

On the bed of the Mwabvi River itself a pale sweep of rinsed river sand cradles the clear water, a shallow wash of ankle-deep rivulets flanked by steep rocky sides. Gnarl-rooted fig trees cling to the gorge and above the crown of rocks, *sterculia* and baobabs show smoke-grey between green foliage.

Golden-banded foresters, butterflies of sapphire blue and chrysanthemum yellow, dance in the shadow of the trees, and an algae-fringed water-scorpion stalks river-boatmen in the rippling shallows. Above, a lazy bateleur swings through the cloud-buttressed sky on the outstretched bracket of his wings.

Mwabvi is best for hikers. The wildlife that threatens bush-innocent townies has been exterminated or eaten - lions, elephants, rhinos - all are long gone. There are still leopard in those romantic looking folds and pleats of rock, but so shy now as not to be a threat. The buffalo, kudu, nyala and sable are still there, if little seen, and the long lush grass, perfect for heavy grazers, is relatively untouched.

Two main tracks pass through the Reserve, meandering along roads that all but vanish just after the rains, the snaking routes of hundreds of bicycles, the predominant form of transport in this area. Who are these myriad cycle riders? Why are they constantly in a protected area? Well, they live here - just the "other side" of the park, and this is the only route to reach the town, the maize mill, the post-office, the clinic... and of course get home again.

The incessant passing of bicycles is a reminder that this park is situated within the most densely populated area of one of the most densely populated countries in all of Africa. Managing parks, with people and for people, is now seen as the key to conservation throughout Africa.

Fish eagles are seldom seen together on the shores of Lake Malawi - outside of the mating season

The powerful mwera, *blowing from the south-east in a night of howling bluster, still brings spray off the waves at sunrise*

An inland sea

Coming to terms with Lake Malawi is not easy. All that huge body of fresh water! It's mind-boggling for anyone brought up in an arid region. The waves, the beach, the crash and splash and the absence of an opposite shore - it's all quite normal, in a fresh and beautiful way, as shorelines are. But after a swim to find there is no salty stickiness is as odd as not seeing shells on the beach.

Scramble over granite boulders tumbled between the sunset and the Lake, listen to the hush and suck of waves on this inland sea, where granite kopjies are studded with baobabs and dassies. The ubiquitous fish eagle calls and a pair of redwing starlings abseil down a rock-face, searching out who knows what. Across the teal-green wrinkled water, the drab splattered rocks on any of the many offshore islands are conjured into a sudden bright confection as they catch the last of the sun.

A silky dark flank heels and slips under the water. The movement was so like that of a seal as to bring confusion - are there freshwater seals? There are salt-water hippos in North Africa.

Oh, of course! An otter! If this fascinating body of water was only a simple stream or even a raucous river. But disguised as a sea this enormous lake misleads and deceives the eye. It's a geological sleight of hand that leaves the viewer ill-equipped for rationality.

Flying clouds

What is it about this Lake that sends most standing on its shores scratching for a poetic quote? Somehow the urge to haul in a literary big gun to launch the assault on the reader's inner eye is irresistible.

The very scale of Lake Malawi reduces the visitor to verbal beggary. Gradually growing accustomed to the idea that it is a lake, and not the sea, somehow makes it more impressive and the graceful frame of distant mist-blue hills contrasting with immediate beach sand, boulders and baobabs is a visual romance.

Often, gazing across the shimmering distance of hazy water, a shifting cloud of smoke can be seen drifting above the waves. Surely it is smoke? What else could hang like a veil above the surface, greyer than mist? A fire on one of the islands springs to mind as a possible explanation with the breeze blowing the smoke shoreward. Or perhaps even a burning cane break, and the smoke drifting across towards the islands.

"It's not smoke at all!" comes the exclamation, "it's a cloud of lake flies!" One of the more amazing aspects of Africa's great lakes, is that the flies which can be such a personal nuisance on other lesser waters elsewhere are heavily concentrated here. The swarms are often a kilometre or so across and almost as deep, millions upon millions of tiny gnats, so small that it's almost difficult to sail through them.

What little is known of these tiny creatures suggests they are as hung up on physical symmetry as we humans are. Physical symmetry is thought to indicate genetic perfection, and the female gnats, like analysts of beauty everywhere, find symmetry attractive.

Kungu fly, *seen here near Bandawe, are both a choking threat to fishermen and a source of food in hard times*

Skyscapes by the Lake, constantly changing hour by hour and throughout the year, provide challenges for photographers

The males apparently congregate for the purpose of proving themselves and each sets about trying to describe a perfect circle in flight. To a mind the size of a gnat's, the perfect flight circle proves perfect symmetry.

The female gnat simply waits on the sidelines of the column of circling males, and when she spots what she judges to be the perfect circle, she dives into the mass of circling males, grabs hold of the male whom she has selected, and flies out of the column and away, still carrying him, to where they can mate.

There is a surprising and altogether different reference to the gnats in a Malawian recipe book, where they are described as "extremely nutritious, high in protein and calcium and containing six times as much iron as ox liver". Certainly when they are blown ashore there is a frenzy of activity as villagers scoop them up with whirling baskets, off the grass and down from the trees. The recipe suggests that they should be cooked with onion, tomato and pounded groundnuts.

The rainbow fish

Stand on the pale biscuit-coloured beaches of Lake Malawi and gaze out over the shimmering expanse of sweet water. Across the gentle heave of deceptively meek waves are the tantalising blue hills of Tanzania or Mozambique, temptresses beckoning with promises of adventure and mystery. Such an easy step. So very near. Such serene, clear and gentle water.

Nature is full of such seductive traps. The lake is known to be extremely volatile. Unwary sailors have been swept away from shore and sustenance in terrifying storms that can last for days, and tossed in waves of five metres or more. Like all fishing nations, Malawians have a deep respect for the lake and its voracious appetite for the lives of boatmen. They snatch a living from the waves and take care not to be snatched in turn.

So far it seems that the people are winning for the lake is slowly running out of *chambo*, the delicious pan-sized fish that, with other smaller lake species, still feeds much of the country. Catches are diminishing and the nets are becoming finer and finer, and even the small and fabulously colourful *mbuna* are being taken now. Though small and bony, food is food.

Mbuna are the famed Lake Malawi *cichlid* fishes, prized throughout the world of tropical fish lovers. As pretty as coral reef beauties, they are much easier to keep since they are fresh-water fish. Just as the land of Malawi is scattered with little isolated mountains or *inselbergs*, so the floor of the lake's shallow shore-line is dotted with little rocky outcrops, each with its own endemic species of *cichlid*. Some say that over 600 species have been identified. The accuracy of that figure may be uncertain, but it is sure that many more have

The waters around Mumbo, top left, and Domwe islands within the Lake Malawi National Park provide a haven for the cichlidae *or* mbuna

The large trees by the Lakeshore have nearly all been felled so nowadays dugouts are carved many miles from the Lake and laboriously transported on rollers or on the backs of pick-ups

not yet been scientifically described.

A plethora of variety does not necessarily mean an abundance of fish, and these little pockets of unique fish fauna are vulnerable to over-fishing. There are an estimated forty thousand traditional fishermen on the Lake who need to feed hungry families. It is simply impossible for the Fisheries Department to monitor and control the catches from these little hand-carved dug-out canoes. Naturally the laws exist, but implementation is impossible.

Yet the pretty fish in their natural habitat are worth a great deal in tourist dollars, and spending several hours head-down in Lake Malawi is an experience few could ever forget.

Although there is a successful commercial trawling operation on the Lake, most fishermen still use the traditional dugouts

Chugging out to the islands, pale rings on the rocks mark earlier higher waterlines, like growth rings in heart wood. In the distance violet and jacaranda-blue storm skies are over-laid with glowing white clouds trailing veils of diaphanous rain.

Domwe Island in the Lake Malawi National Park is, with neighbouring Mumbo Island, one of the best places to see these piscine splendours of Malawi. The island is a bastion of piled boulders melting into liana-hung trees, rock-fig, quinine tree, the elegant upheld arms of a *euphorbia* looking oddly cactus-like in the crowded tropical lushness. Above, a scatter of trumpeter hornbills glissade down the humid air to dip and glide into foliage, while the more mobile visitor is cradled in the rocking lap of sweet water, the colour of antique glass. Further out the lake deepens to a deeper shade, of rich beryl.

Close to the islands the water reveals its fish with startling ease. Far below, a soft blue moonscape of serried rocks fades into pastel shadows, shot through with gleaming fish, satin and shantung and silk in blue and bridal white, peacock and azure, brocaded in silver and velvet black, starred with gold, netted in copper and striped in purple and indigo. A thicket of fish, a storm of tiny glinting bodies, a jewelled rain, a flickering mist-cloud of piscine pulchritude. You can feed scraps of biscuit to these myriad *cichlids*, which hover around like a nebulous sequined waistcoat as tiny eager mouths suck up the fragments like miniature vacuum cleaners.

Danforth Yachting

It's an ill wind...

It is said that as much as eighty percent of Malawi's protein is supplied by fish, and the bulk of that comes from the Lake. With a population of 11 million, that adds up to a lot of fish. The land itself is under great pressure, with deforestation evident and increasing crop cultivation in the catchment areas accelerating erosion and siltation of the lake. Yet Lake Malawi is a remarkably unpolluted body of water, thanks to the lack of any major industries. Indeed, in many places the water of Lake Malawi is so pure that people have used it to top up the batteries in their cars.

Water that is so clean doesn't contain a lot of food for fish, so where does the plethora of piscine fauna come from? That's where our friend, the grey *chiperoni*, comes in. Only, once it reaches the lake, it undergoes a slight personality change. It has dropped most of its moisture on the peaks of Mulanje and Zomba, and with it, the name. Now it's known as the *mwera*, but it has lost none of its force.

Lake Malawi is often deceptively calm but storms can blow up in minutes. In 1999 an expatriate family, in a disabled power boat, was swept hundreds of kilometres up the Lake from Mangochi to Likoma Island. They had disappeared for two weeks. The same wind provides the raison d'etre *for Danforth Yachting's cruise venture based at Cape Maclear*

The wind sweeps in from the south-east - and the long lissom body of Lake Malawi lies exactly along its path. The fierce blow whips up the water, providing vital aeration. As a result Lake Malawi has a wonderfully deep layer of oxygenated water - allowing fish to breathe - which helps to support its weight of piscine biodiversity and productivity. But where's the fish-food?

The food for the inhabitants of the lake is actually at the bottom of this body of water. Lake Malawi is the third deepest in the world - 700 m - and down there the water is devoid of oxygen, and even fish suffocate. But that's where all the heavy nutrients are, washed in by the rivers and dropped in by fishermen and birds and hippos and otters and crocodiles. So the fish can't get at it.

Until the wind blows. Raking along nearly six hundred kilometres of lake, the wind pushes the water up to the northern end. As this weight of water builds up at the "deep" end, it sinks - since water doesn't heap up too successfully. The water underneath it gives way by moving downwards and southwards, scooping up some of that heavy nutrient soup from the bottom and sending it in an underwater wave to the "shallow" end. Scientists call that wave a *seiche*.

So there's a sort of nutrient current that flows against the wind, and an up-welling of food-rich water in the southern end of the Lake. Guess where the best fishing is on Lake Malawi? And, not surprisingly, that's where the greatest population pressure is exerted on the lake.

The Lake Malawi Yachting Marathon takes place each year in July when the mwera *blows hardest*

The event often starts at Sunbird Nkopola Lodge on the southern Lakeshore (right)

It's a marvel that the bitter wind watering the Mulanje cedars and Malawi's mountain tea plantations is the same wind that stirs up the Lake to feed the fish that feed the people. So when David Livingstone was tempted to revise his description of the lake he first named "Lake of Stars" to the less complimentary "Lake of Storms", he accurately if unwittingly reflected the huge debt Malawi owes to that vital but unruly wind.

Likoma Island

If you look at the worm that is Lake Malawi on a map, head down and wriggling south, you'll see the island group of Likoma around about where you would expect to find its stomach if you didn't know much about worms - or stomachs, for that matter.

Chizumulu is the smaller, taller island to the west of long, flat Likoma, and both are almost against the Mozambique shore, well within that country's border. When the lake was carved up by the colonial powers in the 1890's about a hundred kilometres of the eastern lakeshore was handed to Portugal, much to the dismay of the Universities Mission, who had invested considerable effort in Likoma Island. To mollify them, the island group was exempt from the transfer and remained a satellite of the Nyasaland Protectorate.

So it's not surprising that the island of Likoma still has a missionary focus. And the single most remarkable thing about Likoma is certainly the Cathedral. Oliver Ransford, in his book *Livingstone's Lake* describes it as, "... the figure of a knight in prayer beside the Lake", and indeed there is something very Arthurian about this extraordinary building.

Rounding a rocky headland brings first sight of the corrugated iron roof, painted white and now tiring in appearance, for tropical Africa is a harsh environment. The Cathedral was built in the late 1890's; it would not be surprising if there was no roof at all. The building itself seems, from some angles, almost squat, more like a Greek church than an Anglican cathedral.

There is a little cove at the foot of the village of Chipyela. Small stone-built houses in beaten-earth yards, each marked by a perimeter line of round stones, are terraced up the slope and shaded by mango and pod-mahogany trees. The slightly rutted road, whose only motorised traffic comprises the ambulance belonging to St Peter's Hospital, and the army's camouflage-painted jeep, leads upwards.

Round a bend and the cathedral's red-brick cloisters stand arched and cool in the scorching morning heat. But not squat! If this joyful building were not an expression of worship, it would be a work of whimsy. There is certainly the inspiring serenity, the soaring arches to lead the heart higher, the stained glass windows to provide immediate glory. But there is more; there is a delight in shape and space that is playful, a relishing of texture and pattern, a physical pleasure in the play of light and shadow. The building feels part legend, part hymn, and is utterly astounding here on a dusty and crowded African island.

The Universities Mission to Central Africa on their return to the Lake area in 1882, chose Likoma Island as the base for their evangelical efforts. The magnificent St Peter's cathedral, seen here on the right of the aerial picture, left, was completed in 1902

The visual essence of Likoma. The mv Ilala *seen through the island's ubiquitous baobabs and cassava. The vessel still offers the only regular connection between the islands and mainland Malawi*

Statues and interiors like this create an impression of a European cathedral, not of one in the middle of a huge lake in Central Africa!

The elderly verger is there to welcome the stray visitor with a rare and palpable pride. Reverently he opens the sacristy cupboard and brings out the crook of the first Bishop's crozier to admire - carved ivory and garnets set in silver, the Pascal Lamb crowned and triumphant. Hanging on pegs around the room the robes of the servers gleam spotless in bright reflected light, threadbare and frayed, but pressed and ready for Sunday's Mass.

At Mass no visitor, whether worshipper or watcher, can fail to be deeply moved by the beauty of the service. There is little as stirring as many full-throated African voices raised in harmony. The fragile shell of baked brick, shaped soapstone and Victorian iron girders are fleshed out in vibrant sound, African rhythm and Anglican liturgy melding in a celebration of cross-over cultures. And in its own way a celebration of the Cross over cultures.

Likoma, and the northern half of Lake Malawi in general, may become the next focus of tourist interest in Malawi. If the considerable problems of access - to an island in a lake in the middle of Africa - can be overcome, there is on the island sufficient to lure tourists thousands of miles.

Beautiful, completely unspoiled beaches vie for attention with a harsher scenery of stark baobabs in secluded coves. Already there is one remarkable tourist Lodge on the island, Kaya Mawa, a name which simply means "maybe tomorrow"

in Chichewa and conveys well the lack of urgency which tourists find so appealing. It is built in eco-approved style of rock, reeds and blue gum on a tiny promontory, which juts out from the sandy south-west shores of Likoma. Solar panels provide all the electrical requirements.

The impression conveyed by the architecture and the setting is quite magical, of an exotic, secret retreat, indeed just as Kaya Mawa presents itself in what the owners see as Malawi's new market - the wealthy, young and mobile of Europe and the US.

Another tourist facility, also of high standard and pitched at a similar market, Mchenga Nkwichi, has opened just across the narrow divide between Mocambique and Likoma. It lies south of Cobue on the Mocambican shore, within the newly proclaimed Manda Wilderness Reserve. Like Kaya Mawa, it will depend heavily on infrastructural development in and around northern Lake Malawi, especially in air and lake transport.

Kaya Mawa, straddling a tiny peninsula on the southern shore of Likoma, (opposite) offers a memorable eco-tourism experience

The silver sands of Chintheche

The nearest part of 'mainland' Malawi to Likoma is Chintheche. North lies bustling Nkhata Bay and south, the serenity of Bandawe and Kande Beach. It is on this shoreline that the tourism planners of Malawi have been seen most in the past years. Silver beaches of the whitest sand distinguish this stretch as much as the verdant foliage, which in many places rolls down right to the waterline and envelopes tiny rocky coves in a close green embrace. It is a powerfully attractive scenic combination but one where future development will need the most careful control.

Much of the population of the area around Chintheche was displaced in the seventies - to make room for an ambitious pulpwood scheme and harbour facility, all of which eventually came to naught in the cold light of economic appraisal. Their return was encouraged by the democratic government elected in 1994 but that new and augmented population, combined with the impact of the new Lakeshore road allowing easy access to trucks seeking firewood, has meant that they tend to stake their land claims by chopping down the trees. The very same trees which make up the powerful tourism appeal of this area of Lakeshore!

Huge mango trees and nyapini (terminalia) *sweep down to the silver shores of Chintheche*

Dugout fishermen live and fish as they have always done, among the many small lodges found nestling in the coves

On moonless nights the lights carried by the fishermen to attract fish to their nets, create the impression of a well-lit promenade or pier

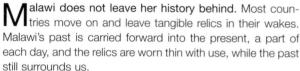

Community Life

Malawi does not leave her history behind. Most countries move on and leave tangible relics in their wakes. Malawi's past is carried forward into the present, a part of each day, and the relics are worn thin with use, while the past still surrounds us.

There are no ancient cities in Malawi. Built of sunbaked clay or rammed earth, and roofed with thatch, houses melt in the rain, gradually returning to the earth. New houses mushroom up, of clay and poles and reed, but they are as old as the hills, old as Lake Malawi itself. The neat little villages we see today are essentially the same as they were when Livingstone first set eyes on his "Lake of Stars".

The villages are charming. Agglomerations of shaggy thatched homes, in some areas with reed-enclosed compounds, neatly swept bare-earth yards and quilted fields behind, are scattered in ribbons along the roads. Glossy goats nose around the *nkhokwe* or maize granary, snooze under the low eaves, or stretch a tethered leg to reach a far, succulent leaf. Occasionally fat-tailed sheep shuffle by, looking depressed and unkempt, tails and ears hanging dejectedly. They look like an unhappy cross between the giddy goats and the edgy village dogs which, thin and rangy, cringe for a morsel at their master's heels, or hunt mice enthusiastically in the undergrowth.

The houses themselves have a fairy-tale quality, the honest simplicity of a child's drawing. Neatly square, each is built on a raised base, just wide enough to walk along, or to sit on comfortably, or to provide shade for three or four somnolent goats.

Sometimes there are marvellous naïve paintings on the walls, more often it's just plain old dried mud, wattle and daub. There is a central door of wood or reeds or rush-matting. On either side are neat six-paned windows, or the walls are embellished by hand-painted patterns along the base. The generous eaves are supported by wonderfully eccentric poles, and the gently sloped roof hangs over to provide welcome shade from the beating sun, or a sheltered space for bunches of tobacco leaves, yellow as kerchiefs, hung up to dry away from the late rains.

Over the reed fences and low thatched roofs, creepers scroll green tendrils and send out furry golden stars on slender stalks. Dark leaved mango trees, or the hippo bulk of baobabs give shade and depth, and a few chickens examine the swept earth like critical sergeant majors. Often a large clay pot rests near the door, the family's water supply. The pots are magnificent, superbly symmetrical despite the lack of potter's wheels. These too are graceful relics of the past, these glorious pots, made today as they were a hundred, a thousand years ago.

Each village has its own scattering of commercial enterprise, a tea room at least, often a grocery store, and a maize mill - the essential *chigayo*, where women stand and wait in autumn groups while their baskets of de-husked corn are transformed into soft white heaps. Business premises, with the exception of tea-rooms which are often simply private homes, have an unmistakable architecture. Above the verandah roof the flat wall of the facade proves the perfect space for advertising the business.

Village huts are still decoratively painted although less so than in the past. This one is on the northern slopes of the Nyika Plateau and shows a giraffe although the animal is thought never to have lived there or anywhere else in Malawi

A typical village market scene

The goats seem to realise the nkhokwe *is full*

Malawians have a gift for whimsical business names. Near Mulanje you will find the *No Money No Friends Maize Mill and Welding Shop*. Many places boast a *Slow But Sure Grocery*, and several small pubs proclaim their services as *The Hangover Clinic*. Among my favourites are the *Pack and Go Coffin Workshop*, the *Honeymoon Bottle Store*, the *Jesus Cares Telephone Exchange* and the disarmingly honest *Money Comes Money Goes Investment Company*. In the graceful little town of Malindi a diminutive grocery store has two inscriptions, one on either side of the door. The first reads *In God We Trust* and beside it *Thank You for Your Calling*. That must have warmed the hearts of all who felt called to work at St Michael's across the road.

Malawians seem to be natural entrepreneurs. Everyone sells something. Individuals set up spontaneous places of purchase beside the road - a few mangoes, a basin of dried fish, a bunch of bananas. It's a long-standing tradition. The first expedition that set out to find Livingstone enraged people on the banks of the Shire by not stopping "to say hello, or to see what we have to sell, or ask if we want to buy something."

In the past decade there has been a flood throughout the country of imported used clothing. Seen here are kaunjika *markets in Mzuzu and Luchenza*

Bananas for sale on the beach at Chintheche, pots by the roadside on the way to Zomba and a tinsmith's wares at Mzuzu market

Market stalls seem endowed with their own excitement. Among the bustle of people, striped plastic bags flutter from poles like pennants. Colourful wares are laid out to view: a riot of bright plastic mugs, clear bags of golden cooking oil, piles of red tomatoes, yellow cucumbers, green beans; pink sweet potatoes, pale cassava roots, podgy grey pumpkins; sheaves of stacked purple sugar cane. In sugar cane season drifts of discarded blue-green leaves litter the road, overlaid with a mat of chewed while pulp. The cane itself is fibrous and indigestible, the juice alone the sweet attraction. Everyone around the country chews the cane and spits out the pith to lie in drifts along the road.

Roads are more than a route from place to place. Each is a congregation point, a source of entertainment, a focus for social interaction. Towards the end of summer, when vegetation is at its riotous extreme, roads provide welcome vistas for the eye as much as easy passage. Roads in rural areas

are more a procession than a convenience for motorised vehicles. And where a good road and a good market place coincide, the result is more like a spontaneous street party.

Making good use of this cheerful Malawian gift are the mobile markets. Groups of entrepreneurs from the bigger towns and cities travel out regularly to rural market places, their goods piled on trucks. Once a week, it seems, a little rural market will suddenly boom, augmented by these itinerant hawkers. The usual home-grown produce is temporarily eclipsed by bright plastic wares, great heaps of second-hand clothing, armloads of *chitenje* cloth, metal cooking pots in gleaming stacks, essential bicycle spares, even batteries

for portable radios. The regularity of the event makes it dependable, the transient nature makes it an occasion to be savoured. It's a remarkably efficient sales technique, and one that seems purely Malawian.

Along the lake, villages have one more component - the fish-drying tables. These seem to be elevated reed mats, some many metres long, the scattered harvest of small silver bodies littered along them. Sometimes an individual home-owner will spread his catch along the ledge around his house, where it throws back the sunlight like bright iron filings. The lake is the major source of protein for Malawi, and while maize is the staple, fish is decidedly the favourite 'relish' for it.

Mzuzu

Mountainous Mzuzu is now famous for its coffee, feted as being particularly fragrant and flavourful. It's a green and folded little town with a certain misty charm, and street verges adorned with banks of flowers, among them roses and masses of soft pink begonia. With their reddish leaves and tall flower stems they are impressively exuberant.

Mzuzu dam, set among plantations and tall *miombo* and *uapaca* forest, is worth exploring though the coolness of the altitude and the generally damp weather discourages water sports, which is perhaps just as well, since this is the town's water supply. Yet it has a Scottish or Canadian feel about it, looking very much in need of tweeded trout-fishermen and a lodge with blazing log fires, or a log-cabin base for launching birch-bark canoes.

Mzuzu itself rests at the northernmost end of the Viphya - where there is just such a splendid lodge at Luwawa - and inland from Nkhata Bay on the Lake. It's essentially a hub for timber products from the extensive plantations on the

The road north to Mzuzu curls through some of the most dramatic highland scenery in the country. This is the aptly named Elephant Rock on the Viphya Plateau

A tiny tobacco farm at nearly 1800m (6000 feet) on the Viphya plateau

The m v Mtendere loads at Nkhata Bay and, above, a roadside scene outside Nkhata Bay

Viphya, coffee and tea closer by, and rubber down by the lake. The administration and shipping centre in the high, healthy air above the coast, products are sent down from there, to be transported south by water at Nkhata Bay to the rail-head at Chipoka, and thence to Blantyre and the Mozambique coast.

The proposed pulp mill and paper factory to process the timber from the Viphya plantations never materialised. That's extremely good for the Lake, since it's the lack of major industry that maintains the Lake's pristine condition. And the plantations and forests around Mzuzu provide lovely walks and a wonderland for bird watchers.

Lilongwe

Lilongwe is remarkable for several reasons, and the first is that it has virtually no history. Like anywhere else in Malawi it can claim to have had early stone-age hunter-gatherers - after the plentiful game on the plateau. Later these were chased into the hills by iron-age agriculturalists, who knew good farming land when they saw it. Then came the militant Yao, followed by the warlike Angoni, and certainly slaves were taken from this area, as elsewhere in Malawi. But none of this is unique. Where places like Nkhotakota, Mangochi or Blantyre have names that resonate with historical associations, Lilongwe has none. No-one pivotal was born here, no great battle was fought, no movement started, no vital trade route established. It's almost as if Lilongwe was chosen as the capital for its snowy character reference - it is a city without a past.

In the Victorian era, Lilongwe, then part of Central Angoniland, was administered by a District Commissioner

The private sector has followed the lead by Government in setting high architectural standards. Seen here are Kang'ombe House and a Ministry building

based at Dedza. In 1904 district headquarters moved to the *boma* in Lilongwe, and long after independence, in 1975, Lilongwe was declared the capital of Malawi. And this is where the second most remarkable aspect of modern Lilongwe came about; its basic town plan.

Work began in the early 1970s, the new Capital City having been laid out by South African architects and town planners with an eye to future expansion. It was a potential recipe for boredom. In Australia the city of Canberra, also a purpose-

built capital, was laid out in the usual grid pattern - all straight lines and regulation sized plots of ground. In South Africa the new mining city of Welkom was hailed as advanced for its lack of traffic lights and plentiful open spaces, but the grid pattern and the regulation plots were still fundamental to their plans. Lilongwe, by a design true to the village pattern, managed to escape this regimented feel.

A map of Lilongwe's streets is satisfyingly reminiscent of some of the Stone Age line-paintings found in shelters around Dedza - a combination of abstract lines and curves that charm the eye even though they can bewilder the visitor. It's a wonderful organic plan, one that caters to the contours of the land and its requirements. Very few plots of land are the same size, and the result is a sense of pleasing individualism.

The capital city is spread over a large hilly area, and the natural drainage lines and seeps that run off the high ground are, sensibly, left undeveloped. In places these are still quite well-wooded, and provide fingers of apparent wilderness through the city. It's a green ideal that many first-world cities,

or at least their environmentally aware citizens, would aspire to. Even in the commercial centre of the city there is a feeling of being out in the bush. For instance, there is a longcrested eagle that frequents a street light on Presidential Way, and at night the whoop of spotted hyenas sounds eerily up the cricket-creaking *dambos*, as they stroll the moonlit city centre. These are the self-appointed, unpaid members of the city refuse collection department, and don't seem to suffer any lack.

Lilongwe itself has two faces, Old Town, and City Centre. Old Town stays much as it was, and retains some of the atmosphere of the original bustling village, while to the north are the serene modern government ministries on Capital Hill, with the City Centre, graced with tall trees and open spaces, below.

Lilongwe's huge purpose-built tobacco auction floors (opposite) provide an economic raison d'etre *for Liongwe's development and growth*

The seat of government in Malawi is Capital Hill where custom built Ministries grace a splendid hill top site

Mangochi

To most Malawians, Mangochi is a holiday centre. The town serves the many resorts that are bunched along the southern shores of the lake of which the best known internationally are Sunbird Nkopola Lodge, Club Makokola and Sun 'n Sand. These same resorts provide for Malawi's favourite democratic process, the "workshop". All major decisions seem to require a workshop and Mangochi is undoubtedly the workshop capital of Malawi. It is also the main base for deep lake fishing but workshopping is probably the dominant industry in the district.

Palm-shaded Mangochi straddles the broad Shire River on that short stretch between draining Lake Malawi and swelling to form Lake Malombe. A few kilometres north, where, more than a century ago, Mponda's town faced across to Fort Johnston, the gap between Mangochi Mountain and the Namizimu range can be clearly seen. This was the southernmost gateway from Lake Nyasa through Portuguese territory to the east coast and Kilwa, the important distribution depot of slaves from the country. Livingstone mentions Mponda's town in 1861.

The palm and the baobab set the scene for many visitors to present day Mangochi

Seen here are the splendid Mlambe golf course at Club Makokola and the beachfront at Sunbird Nkopola Lodge

Sir Harry Johnston, the first administrator of the Protectorate thirty years later, described Mponda as "a very repellent type of Yao robber, alternately cringing and insolent". Mponda's impressions of Johnston were preserved for us by Johnson-without-the-t, the missionary pioneer Archdeacon William Percival Johnson who records that Mponda seemed both puzzled and impressed. "Who is this little man," he is said to have remarked, "that comes and talks with authority?"

Mponda was a Yao chief and a slave trader, and his town was perfectly situated to control the settlers' communication route between the Lake and the Shire, and to keep a distant eye on the slave route through the southern end of the Rift escarpment to the coast.

Fort Johnston began as a little encampment in an "uninhabited reed wilderness" opposite Mponda's town, set up when trouble between Mponda and other Yao chiefs interrupted communications to and from the Lake. A sequence of attack and counter attack followed, and Mponda, despite an earlier treaty, sided with "Zarafi" or Jelasi, a powerful chief living on Mangochi Mountain. Only when Mponda and Jelasi were subjugated - the latter some three years later - and Fort Mangochi established on the site of Jelasi's town, could Johnston turn his attention to the persistent problem of Mlozi in the north.

Harry Johnston's "reed wilderness" was probably uninhabited because the spot was full of mosquitos. In establishing the fort, a moat was thought essential. This, being below river level, was naturally full of stagnant water all year round - a superb breeding ground for both mosquitoes and bilharzia snails. Not surprising then, that old Fort Johnston was declared "unhealthy" and the fort was moved to slightly higher, healthier ground across the river. A feature of the narrows and shallows where the second Fort Johnston was built, on the same bank and downstream of Mponda's, was a sand /sediment bank referred to as "the bar". Certain early gravestones in the Mangochi cemetery include the enigmatic inscription "died at the bar". This is a geographic locational reference and not an inference that the deceased was a dipsomaniac...The establishment of a more permanent Fort Johnston began some miles south in 1897, and the town was laid out by the second administrator, Alfred Sharpe.

A SIKH SENTRY AT FORT JOHNSTON, BRITISH CENTRAL AFRICA
FROM A WATERCOLOUR DRAWING BY H.H. JOHNSTON. C.B.

One of the earliest examples of town planning in Central Africa, it shows that Sir Alfred Sharpe, too, was a man of many parts. The town, and the district, were renamed Mangochi by Dr Kamuzu Banda, in 1971.

So modern Mangochi is distanced by a few kilometres from the early settlements of Mponda's town and Fort Johnston. With its elegant sweep of bridge across the Shire and the unmistakably colonial Clock Tower, she feels distanced, too, from the memory of slave sticks, brutality and war. Basking in the still heat of the valley, the undersides of her palm leaves marbled with the shifting reflections of moving water, Mangochi has a romantic charm and there is a faintly mischievous tingle to the air.

Interestingly, Mangochi has cherished some of the relics of her past. Near the Clock Tower is the Lake Malawi Museum, housed in what used to be the Lake Nyasa Yacht and Gymkhana Club. It consists of a neatly maintained collection of items ranging from stone-age artifacts to the original steam engine from that dapper little steamer, the m.v. *Chauncy Maples*. She, like most of the ships that plied the Lake, was carried overland, piece by painstaking piece,

an amazing 3500 packages in all. She was assembled at Mponda's in 1901 though the deeper water at Malindi was needed for her final fitting out. Unbelievably, perhaps, she still plies the clear, clean waters of the lake, over 100 years later. The gunboat *Guendolen*, famed for the "Naval Victory on Lake Nyasa" at the start of World War I when she put out of action the only German gunboat on the Lake, was also assembled at Fort Johnston. The bridge of the *Guendolen* has been reconstructed in the museum, and one of her Hotchkiss guns stands at the base of the Clock Tower.

Opposite: Sir Harry Johnston's own drawing of a Sikh sentry at the eponymously named Fort Johnston.

The calm serenity of the beach at Club Makokola is in marked contrast to the embattled early days of the District

That redoubtable 'Lady of the Lake', the m v Chauncy Maples

The market in Zomba, with its profusion of colour among the fruit and vegetable stalls, is well worth the short detour

Zomba

It seems almost impossible to separate Zomba from Sir Harry Hamilton Johnston, Commissioner of the then newly proclaimed Protectorate of Nyassaland Districts. Johnston chose to be based at Zomba for at least two reasons. The first was that a base had already been established there by his predecessor. Consul A G S Hawes had chosen Zomba for its proximity to a slave route, since this was the main concern of his appointment.

The original Scottish Mission might have been established where Zomba is today, had it not been decided that the proximity of that very slave route made the place too dangerous, and they settled instead at Blantyre. However, John Buchanan, an "agriculturalist" with the Mission in 1876, did not scare easily and four years later he moved to Zomba and, with his brothers, set up coffee and sugar plantations. Buchanan built the consulate for Hawes, and stood in as vice-consul when Hawes took leave. It was during this time that Buchanan declared the area a British Protectorate in the face of apparent Portuguese interest.

In today's specialist world, it's hard to comprehend that this was all regarded as quite normal. That a gardener, brought from Scotland to "assist the Mission in horticulture" fourteen years earlier, could be left in political control without anyone raising so much as an eyebrow. That the actual builder of the Residency should hold the reins of government. Another remarkable impact that Buchanan had on the

country was that it was he who initiated the introduction of coffee plants to Central Africa.

For Johnston, the twin facts that he generally disliked missionaries, and that the community of planters and traders disliked him, may have played a role in his preferring the isolation of Zomba to the everyday irritations of more populous Blantyre. However, one suspects that the second major reason for the choice was purely aesthetic. In *The Story of My Life* Harry Johnston mentions Blantyre, saying "...that place was pretty, but Zomba was superb."

Harry Johnston's opinion of Zomba is still valid today. Zomba is still superb. Johnston's old Residency is now the Hotel Masangola, where efforts are being made to add to the remarkable architecture by recapturing the colonial ambience of Johnston's times. One can still trace the terraced gardens, laid out, as were the neighbouring National Botanical Gardens, by that "eccentric old gentleman" Alexander Whyte, Johnston's Naturalist and Scientific Horticulturalist.

Eccentric as many of Johnston's administrators (and indeed Johnston himself) seemed, it's clear that almost without exception everyone who came to Central Africa at that time, missionaries, planters and civil servants, were extraordinary people. Independent, strong-willed and, for the most part, multi-talented, it's hardly surprising that these men occasionally appeared a little odd, for they were certainly not average people.

The distinctively styled Hotel Masongola in Zomba was built in 1886 as the official residence for the first Commissioner

The memorial to the King's African Rifles whose First Battalion, now the Malawi Rifles, has always been based here, stands guard at the entrance to the municipality

And Zomba is not an average town. Backed against the side of Zomba mountain, looking out over the wide Phalombe plain towards the distant misty bulk of Mulanje, the setting is magical. The picturesque town has grown organically with no rigid grid pattern, just a graceful meander to the streets as they follow the original footpaths. Runoff from the heights of Zomba tumbles down ferned and mossy groins to form lively streams that thread through town. These, as much as the vast and stately blue-gums and the lush mountain flank, give Zomba a particular charm.

Apart from the visual delight of the place, Zomba remains a centre of considerable importance as the headquarters of many government departments. The army is headquartered here, the National Herbarium, the University of Malawi and Chancellor College, the Geological Survey and the National Archives, among others.

Above Zomba the Ku Chawe hotel boasts a remarkable baronial hall style perfectly in keeping with its unique mountain-top setting

Blantyre

Malawi's city of Blantyre was established in "... the most populous part of the country...", so it's no wonder that the centre still is the largest and busiest in Malawi, and the major commercial centre. Blantyre was in fact a thriving metropolis before Harare or Nairobi had a modern building to their names. Founded in 1876 by the Established Church of Scotland, Blantyre was about a day's tramp from the point on the Shire where the Kapichira Falls stopped boats from going further.

To the weary Scottish missionaries, clothed from ankle to wrist and chin in several layers of hot and scratchy woollen flannel, the drop in temperature as they trudged sore-footed up to the Shire Highlands must have been a huge relief. Some almost imagined these lovely rolling hills and the crisp night air to be like Scotland, and named it in honour of Livingstone's birthplace.

In 1891 Harry Johnston describes the town as "... clean red roads, neat brick houses, purple mountains and much greenery..." Altogether a happier picture than the vague uneasiness inherent in Laurens van der Post's description some sixty years later.

The CCAP Church of St Michael and All Angels stands as magnificent centrepiece in the original Mission grounds. It remains as much an architectural wonder as a Presbyterian aberration; as though the missionary passage through the tropics had imbued a measure of happy, even eccentric,

The main thoroughfare is Victoria Avenue. At the southern end of this main street is the Old Town Hall

Behind the old boma *area the earliest Asian trading houses set up business in patioed courtyards*

Catholicism in their attitude to the stern task of church building. It is said that more than eighty different types and sizes of bricks were burned for the construction of this remarkable building – by churchmen devoid of all architectural training.

Today, Blantyre seems to blend the picturesque charm of Zimbabwe's hill-top town of Mutare, the bustle of Kenya's Mombasa, and the squalor of South Africa's Germiston, with a sense of muted excitement. It has an energetic, chaotic feel as it straggles through its landmark hills, its pavements choked with the street vendors as much as their customers, its streets as full of mini-buses, pick-up trucks and cars. A high proportion of the traffic has four-wheel drive.

Fragments of Blantyre retain a flavour of earlier days. Lower Sclater Road curves downhill from the market area

towards the spritely stream of the Mudi, and is still lined with quaintly characterful, if unassuming, Victorian buildings. It's a great shame that these charming old trading houses will no doubt soon be knocked down and replaced by modern buildings. Africa has a great love of all things new and scant regard for anything which is not. Historical buildings are still not seen as an inheritance, but as a hand-me-down, a sign of poverty.

Blantyre has grown very fast in the past twenty years, perhaps most in the last ten years, and that growth has been well-founded on the commerce introduced first by the earliest traders such as Mandala, as the African Lakes Company was locally known. The Mandala headquarters is the oldest building in Malawi having been completed in 1885. It has been declared a National Monument by the Department of Antiquities.

Opposite, a view of Chiradzulu Mountain from Mpingwe in Limbe

Mandala House is the oldest building in Malawi. It was built by the Moir brothers as the headquarters for their African Lakes Corporation enterprise

The Church of St Michael and all Angels is an impressive structure with over 80 types of bricks created by amateur architects to enhance its decorative appeal

The wealth is in the soil

Hovering in the misty heat haze above Malawi's Shire River Valley is the Thyolo Escarpment. Compared to the heat of the valley, the higher ground is wonderfully cool. In fact it's still pretty warm and with a tropical rainfall that keeps the earth moist. It's ideal tea growing country.

The little centre of Thyolo is only 40 kilometres out of Blantyre, but it looks like a different world. Here tea plantations cling like emerald moss to the contours of the red earth and skim the sensuous flanks of hills. Fringes of trees break the even sweep of green - a palisade of pines, the broad blaze of flat-crowned flame trees, the regular deep green of a line of Golden Oak drawn like a gauze screen at the end of a field. Where the ground is too steep or too wet the natural bush has been left, a frieze of exuberant forest with palm trees, acacias, wild bananas and tree ferns in robust diversity. The surrounding manicured monoculture gives this wild exuberance a horticultural flavour, as if planned by some skilled landscape architect.

The tea estates are so richly picturesque that one longs to be a painter. The even rows of bushes squared off like a quilted coverlet; the clear pure green of leaves against the raw clay roads sunken between the fields, each track neat as a street, glowing ochre-orange or glistening red. Here and there the smooth dome of a boulder breaks the surface of the tea bushes, and stands proud of the symmetry like a granite rock in a raked gravel garden. Above are Turneresque skies full of majestic clouds: steam white, lilac and slate grey set against Wedgewood and cobalt blues.

In the rolling green swell of lawns of tea, neat sheds and stores, whitewashed and gleaming in the rich sunlight, staff housing is set in pretty little gardens and the main estate offices shelter under a canopy of flame trees. Around tractors and trailers, and past tarpaulined picking stations, glimpses can be had of the roofs and chimneys of the tea drying sheds and packing factory.

The road dips through a groin of wild forest, submarine green and tinkling with water, swings round above the bank of a farm dam, and enters a thick screen of stately old tees. A guest bungalow, one of many which are available to the visitor in Thyolo and Mulanje, sprawls graciously on a grassy knoll, surrounded by a gloriously colourful garden and shaded by huge flowering trees. Beyond are wrap-around views of lush and falling land under tall skies, with Mount Mulanje a purple patch in the clouds.

There is something very special about tea. It doesn't deserve to be ground to powder and put in convenient little bags. It's essentially a slow and graceful product of generous serenity and beauty. Yet tea is not Malawi's prime agricultural earner, nor was it ever the initial choice of farmers in this greenly glowing country.

Malawi has always been cultivated. For almost as long as man has been around, crops have been grown. When Livingstone first saw Malawi, he was impressed by the fields of cotton and local tobacco, introduced from America, perhaps three or four centuries ago now, by the Portuguese. In 1896 Sir Harry Johnston remarked "Not even slave trade devastations

Tea is Malawi's second biggest export crop, grown mostly in Thyolo and Mulanje

The crop has seen such major price falls in recent years that several plantations have opened their guest houses like this one, above, at Satemwa Estate, to tourism

Fertiliser is applied by special crop-spraying aircraft and the 'table' is pruned to maintain a workable plucking height

Sugar is grown by Illovo on its two huge estates at Nchalo on the Lower Shire and Dwangwa on the Lakeshore while several groups of smallholders and individuals have also started planting cane

Rubber has been grown for well over a century at the Vizara Estate, near Nkhata Bay

and the continual warfare between tribe and tribe for the past two hundred years have succeeded in destroying agriculture…."

One early missionary planter admitted that he was to learn about farming from the native Malawians, and not to teach as he had expected. However, those enthusiastic followers of Livingstone did bring cultivars from the Asian subcontinent, England and Scotland to boost subsistence farming to commercial agriculture, and they began with coffee.

In Johnston's somewhat self-laudatory *Report on the First Three Years Administration of the Eastern Portion of the British Central Africa Protectorate* published in 1894, coffee was listed as the second highest export after ivory, but it earned only a sixth of the income. The highest export figure reached was two million pounds at the turn of the century, when, with the attack of disease, the market collapsed, and coffee gradually gave way to tea, cotton and tobacco. There was one notable experiment by the African Lakes Corporation, with rubber, at Vizara south of Nkhata Bay. Cultivation was never widespread, because rubber's high rainfall needs effectively restrict its growth to the proximity of rain forest, but to this day Vizara Estate still exports while supplying much of Malawi's domestic needs.

But long before all that, the redoubtable John Buchanan, the canny young gardener from Drummond Castle in Perthshire, had seen the value of agricultural diversification, and had been experimenting with another crop which was to play a strong role in Malawi's economy, sugar.

He began in 1881 beside the Mulunguzi Stream at the foot of Zomba mountain, with a few experimental acres of cane and a small hand-made wooden sugar mill. The following year he built a second mill in Blantyre and improved the one at Zomba, but, since the locals had not yet acquired a taste for refined sugar, he made a note that although production amounted to a most promising two tons in 1882, with "no extensive consumption, the cultivation has to be kept in small bounds". One wonders what he would say now of the rolling landscapes of waving cane of Sucoma beside Elephant Marsh or on the Lakeshore around Dwangwa!

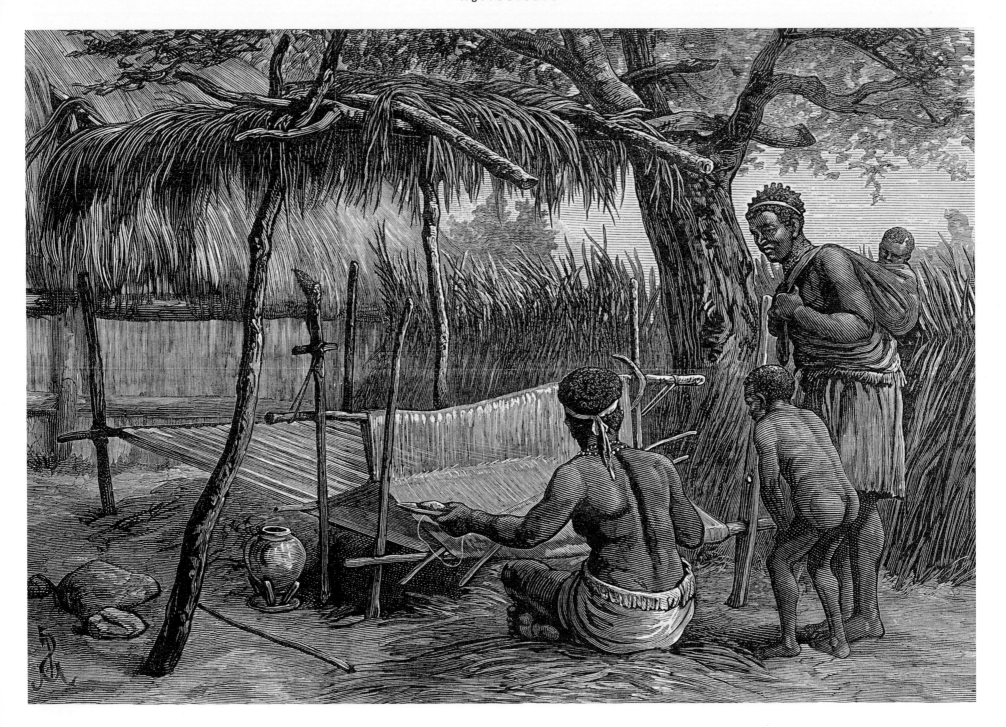

Livingstone considered Malawi to be perfect for cotton growing and found the crop already cultivated. Opposite is an engraving from the Illustrated London News *of 1868 showing "cotton weaving among the Manganja"*

The skill was lost in the face of cheap imports and nowadays the ubiquitous khonde *tailor, working with locally grown and manufactured cloth, faces a similarly threatened future*

Interestingly, not much is said of attempts to grow cotton, though in Harry Johnston's time a coarse cotton cloth was successfully woven in rural villages, a skill that seems to have been entirely lost. It seems the flood of fine soft calico that came in with the missionary-traders took the need out of the exercise. In modern Malawi, too, imports have again crippled home efforts – today it's the tidal wave of second-hand clothing that has swamped the local industry. Affecting not only cotton production and milling, the wonderful Malawian tailors, too, have a hard time making ends meet in the face of the "bend-down boutique" and its affordable garments. 'kaunjika' It's a very real pity; in less modern times everyone in southern Africa knew that the finest quality cotton cloth came from Malawi.

The mainstay of Malawi's economy for years has been tobacco. Needless to say, that probably-pipe-puffing Scott, John Buchanan, was in the forefront again. Malawi's *labu* was the yellow flowered tobacco, and the Buchanan brothers introduced the pink flowered Virginia variety. This was more suited to cigars than the "wild" kind, used mostly as snuff or in communal pipes. By 1892 the Buchanan brothers were marketing their own tobacco products in the Shire Highlands - cut tobacco, choroots and cigars - and began exporting the following year.

Hynde and Starke were the next big names in tobacco, pioneering the tenant farming method, one which still plays a vital role in Malawi's economy. Over the next thirty years tobacco became Malawi's prime revenue earner, hardly surprising when tobacco proved to be more than twenty

Tobacco seed, which is remarkably
fine, is first planted in seed beds
and then transplanted in September
and October with sufficient water
to nurture the plant until the first
rains arrive

Burley tobacco is grown
extensively throughout
Malawi by village farmers

times more profitable than cotton and nearly sixty times higher than maize! Malawi is famed now as the world's largest burley tobacco grower – that's the type grown mainly by smallholders from Phirilongwe to Rumphi with the bigger estates generally favouring the more capital intensive flue cured tobacco. Huge purpose-built auction floors in both Lilongwe and Blantyre, and now Mzuzu too, administer the seasonal sale of Malawi's huge crop to international end users - in a brisk and amazingly efficient exercise of the power of demand over supply.

Simple statistics underscore the country's dependence on the soft golden leaf:

In 1999 the export of over 147 thousand tonnes of tobacco earned Malawi a staggering US$272 million, which comprised 15% of GDP and 58% of Malawi's foreign earnings.

An estimated 1.59 million people were, in that year, employed in growing tobacco, no less than 45% of the national labour force.

There is no crystal ball to gaze into, and tell the future of tobacco in the face of the vociferous worldwide anti-smoking campaign. Certainly the industry in Malawi will have to change,

and that will not be easy when the country so clearly has a tobacco dependency. Indeed many commentators speak of a 'policy paralysis' in the face of these very real threats.

A recent economic analysis of Malawi's tobacco industry by the Economic Studies and Strategies Unit of PricewaterhouseCoopers in Australia puts the dilemma succinctly and more forcefully;

"With such a significant impact on the country's economic prosperity and well-being, it is critical to the future development of the nation that its tobacco industry - particularly the growing, processing, handling and export of tobacco leaf – is sustained and enhanced. Loss of this important economic crop would require immediate action in Malawi to substitute other economic activities and these alternative activities would need to provide the wide regional economic benefits that are currently available from the growing and export of tobacco leaf."

An aerial view of a tiny farm near Zomba neatly prepared for the onset of the rains, maize and tobacco planting

Burley tobacco seen drying under the eaves of a village house

Perhaps the shift to a world health-fixation will give a boost to the promising organic farming so well suited to Malawi, perhaps Malawi will demonstrate conclusively that it has exactly the right climate and soils for niche crops like paprika. Perhaps the embryonic tourism industry will survive the benign neglect of the authorities and, in more enterprising private hands, prove to be the economic leader it so richly deserves to be. Who knows?

The larger estates, such as this one in Phirilongwe, use large 'multi-storey' barns for drying burley tobacco

Both chillies and paprika show potential in the crop diversification so sought by Malawi in the face of the threats to its tobacco-based economy

Flowing sedately south from Mangochi, the Upper Shire broadens into Lake Malombe

The River

The Shire River, known around the 16th century to Portuguese explorers as the Cherim, has its source in Lake Malawi. On a map the lake looks like a open-mouthed caterpillar, dangling head down. From its nose a thread suspends the distorted ball of Lake Malombe just out of reach of the snapping jaws. The thread is the first stretch of the Shire, a wide and handsome river, perennially carrying Lake Malawi's abundant waters away to the sea.

It's not a long journey, somewhere between five and six hundred kilometres, which is not very far in Africa, but it's a journey of great variety and interest. For the last third of the Shire's independent journey before it merges with the Zambesi, the river leaves Malawi, becoming part of the border with Mozambique in the far south, so we will follow it only from its source to where it leaves the interior, just below Chiromo in the south.

It's interesting that countries and ships were spoken of as female while rivers and lakes were not assigned a sex, yet the Shire has decidedly female attributes. Like the Goddess Athena who leapt fully armed from Zeus' head, the Shire springs from Lake Malawi in full flow. No tottering little runnels of spring water feeling their tentative way downhill for Madame Shire. Here is a full-bodied voluptuous river, mature at birth, lovely and completely self-assured. She sweeps past Mangochi like a stately matron, indifferent to the town and the arched ornament of its new bridge.

Very soon she pauses to make a lake of her own, Malombe, a vast spill of water spreading across the level

*An open bill stork by the shores of
Lake Malombe*

*The Shire passes Mvuu
Wilderness Lodge in Liwonde
National Park*

plains, as she feels for the almost imperceptible western arm of the great Rift to take her southwards to the sea. Looking down on Lake Malombe from the heights of Mangochi Forest Reserve, it's hard to believe that this impressive spread of water could ever dry up. It did in 1915, and could again given a prolonged drought, or slight tectonic action from the still malleable crust we call solid earth. Until then it's a haven for wildfowl and, like Lake Malawi and all other waters in the country, an essential source of protein for the multitude living along the banks.

Through the Park

Where Malombe shrinks to become the Shire once more, the river enters Liwonde National Park. This too is flat land, a wide flood plain bordered by distant hills, the purpling edge of the Rift. Here the Shire looks much as it did in Livingstone's day. The banks are fringed by palms and fever trees, emerald green water-grass carpets the shallows where herds of elephants splash and wallow. Groups of hippos form rock-like clusters in the current, with only an occasional snort or splash during the heat of the day, their contented honking mostly reserved for the cooler dawn and dusk. A crocodile drifts past like a half-submerged log and another basks motionless on a pale sand-spit beside a reed bed.

The shot-silk surface of the river reflects towering white clouds, and mirrors the bellies of water birds winging slowly by - egrets, open-billed storks, and skeins of cormorants their beaks slightly open as they fly. An African skimmer cuts the reflection like a pair of tailor's shears. On the bank kingfishers perch on reeds or overhanging branches, and bee-eaters sweep and dart from the shade of a baobab. Weavers' golden wings flash like feathered flame in creeper-hung shrubs. The diminutive shape of Dickinson's kestrel is back-lit on the blunt tip of a dead palm tree, and a cormorants roost has turned an elegant *sterculia* into a stark white skeleton in a small patch of ammonia-scented moonscape.

If you let the current carry you silently beside the bank, you will hear the serried calls of birds echo down the sun-

dappled distance, coucal, wood-dove, palm-thrush, oriole and tropical bou-bou. You may catch a glimpse of regal sable, necks arched to bear the weight of twin scimitar horns, faces dramatic as charcoal and wood-ash, or meet the brown inquisitive stare of furry water-buck.

Gradually the re-appearance of dugout canoes and the beautifully constructed fish-traps show that the park has been left behind, and the river sweeps on to the barrage at the town of Liwonde. The barrage was built in 1965 to exert some control on the level of the river, essential for the country's hydro-electric power stations. It seems almost impossible but this barrage can, to limited extent, regulate the water level in Lake Malawi. This is an indication of the flatness of the river-valley. The ground falls by a two scant metres between the exit from the lake and the barrage itself, over seventy kilometres away.

From Liwonde through Mpimbe and on to Matope, place names well known in the old days when ships like the Adventure and the Charles Janson were brought piecemeal

In the rainy season huge floating islands drifting down river can cause havoc at the Liwonde Barrage which aims to introduce some control over Lake and Lower River levels

Hippos are as common on the Shire River as anywhere in Africa

overland from Chikwawa and assembled at these points. From here, going upstream on the River Shire was relatively easy. Between Matope and Liwonde the ground rises by a gentle seven metres, and the river is wide and generous. But at Matope the ground starts to fall away in a series of steep and jagged steps. Over the next seventy or so kilometres, the bed of the Shire drops by four hundred metres.

Mpatamanga

This is the mid-section of the Shire, and it's hard not to think of it as the river's mid-life crisis. The easy flat land gives way to broken rocky outcrops, and the river is forced into narrow and boulder-strewn channels, splashing and leaping like a hooked fish. It plunges and foams down seven sets of rapids and two waterfalls before it reaches Mpatamanga, where the old road from Mwanza crossed the Shire on its way past Chileka Airport to Blantyre. Two of Malawi's hydro-electric power stations are along this stretch of wildly plunging river.

Mpatamanga Gorge, not long ago, was a favourite spot for Blantyre's Sunday picnic parties. Now the road is little used, and the beautiful forest reserve is thinning rapidly to feed the city's undiminished need for charcoal. Charcoal trucks stand waiting at the boom on the western side of the old metal Bailey bridge, where the policeman on duty proudly

Despite the River's deceptively docile appearances in the aerial pictures, white water rafting, so popular on the Zambezi, has never been attempted on it

announces that he is "working in collaboration with the Forestry Department on the charcoal." An endless stream of bicycles threads the hump-backed dirt-road between here and town; westward empty, eastward loaded down with two huge stuffed and tattered bags spilling black chunks as bent and glistening backs push the bikes uphill to town. Such thankless work for such meagre profit, and such locust-like devastation to the forest!

But Mpatamanga Gorge itself is still magnificent. The Shire, cappuccino brown, is squeezed between grey rocks, marbled and swirled and streaked with cream. Strong straight fracture lines offset the wild chaos of leaping water

and static marbling. Rock-breaker figs send roots taut as tendons down the kranzes, and tendrils of creepers strung with leaves shift in the updraft of air. Serene tree trunks soar above the tumbled rocks and tumbling water and a china blue sky seals in the baking heat. A single martial eagle twirls aimlessly by on lazy wings.

Plunging and bucking like a runaway horse, the Shire battles the restraining rocks. If you creep away from the blazing sun into the water-cold shade near the river, you feel that energy shuddering below. The rushing river makes you feel that you yourself are moving.

On either side of the noisy flow, the rocky ground jags upwards, clothed in wonderfully inaccessible forest relics; knob-thorn, mountain seringa, and that wonderfully named *brachystegia*, the Prince-of-Wales' feathers. In their dappled shade are clumps of *sansevieria*, robust aloes and dark leafed *dracaenas*. Lilac flowered *plectranthus* fill the shadows, starred with flashes of a tiny scarlet hibiscus bloom, and salmon pink witchweed crowds the sunlight. Dried and folded, the big star-shaped leaves of the *sterculia* tree litter the path like scraps of fine leather, gleaming earthy tan above and soft suede under, creamy as river foam.

Kapichira Falls

From Mpatamanga the Shire covers almost as many rapids in the next 15 kilometres as she did between Matope and the Gorge, culminating in the glorious Kapichira Falls. These were the falls that echoed the disappointment Livingstone felt at Cahora Bassa on the Zambezi, the cataracts that put paid to his dream of "God's Highway" to the interior. Kapichira was less daunting, and, as though to make it even less of a hindrance, Livingstone named it for his friend Murchison. However, the Murchison Falls on the Nile were named first, so these became the Murchison Rapids until renamed after independence.

The falls themselves were once declared a National Monument, and Majete Wildlife Reserve's boundary was extended a little to include them. This double protection was simply not enough to preserve the falls as Livingstone saw them. The third hydro-electric station was built there in the last years of the twentieth century. The wild, majestic spill of the Shire is now trammelled by a stone-clad bund thrown right across the river. It's hard not to wonder at the wisdom of basing all three of the country's power sources on a river known to be erratic in flow. Another series of years such as those that produced the drying up of Lake Malombe in 1915 could cause a country-wide electrical brown-out.

Between the Kapichira Falls and the bridge at Chikwawa the Shire regains her old character. She shakes out her skirts and settles down to a more expansive, less harried existence. It seems incredible that this swiftly flowing muscular river could have squeezed through those bottle-neck cataracts at all. Once more on gentle, open land, the river loops like a giant serpent across the rolling green valley. Above the Chikwawa bridge, the outer sweep of the curving river has carved away the red earth, leaving a tall terra-cotta bank, perfect for bee-eaters to excavate nest holes. The carmine

The road to the south crosses the Shire at Chikwawa. Carmine bee-eaters nest in the high banks here

Most of Malawi's best cattle farms are found in the fertile Lower Shire valley

White faced ducks can take to the wing nearly vertically

bee-eater in particular is said to nest here in scores.

Overlooked by the Shire Highlands and the Thyolo escarpment, the river settles into the lowland hush of heat, humidity and reeds. This is the fertile alluvial plain where Livingstone recognised cotton growing. He thought of the vast industrial machines of his Scottish childhood and saw a profitable future for the land. Today cotton has given way to sugar. The Sucoma canefields now stretch for 25 km down the west bank to Nchalo, and from the Shire to the borders of Lengwe National Park

Elephant Marsh

Opposite Sucoma the river slows even more and spills across the flood plain in a number of minor channels and marshy areas. This is the fabled Elephant Marsh. Rankin described it in 1883: "As far as the eye could see, to the base of the highlands, stretched out a vast plain, covered with low sedge grass and reeds. Here and there, in the distance, were clumps of wild palms. Great ant heaps stood up in every direction among cane thickets. From the paddle-box we could see innumerable herds of animals - gazelles, antelopes, buffaloes and elephants. ... (This is) one of the finest hunting-grounds in the world, and well worthy of a visit from European sportsmen."

European "sportsmen" were already well acquainted with Elephant Marsh. The opinionated and egocentric Faulkner, almost twenty years earlier, apparently joined the search for Livingstone as an excuse to take pot-shots at anything that

*The sugarcane fields of SUCOMA
at Nchalo*

**The light at Elephant Marsh is particularly
pleasing for photography**

moved in this paradise, counting the number of animals he wounded with as much pride as those he killed. He so enjoyed himself that he came back for more wholesale slaughter in 1876 (and stayed to father a son before coming to an unhappy end).

Elephant Marsh was the country's very first nature reserve, proclaimed in 1897. Already the numbers of game had dropped alarmingly since Livingstone first set eyes on it some forty years before, and despite the protection of being proclaimed a Government Game Reserve, the last elephant was shot in 1901. The park was de-proclaimed ten years later.

A century on, Elephant Marsh is still a place of wonder. Some people talk of the "atmosphere" of the place, others try to find words to describe "the light". Seen from the top of the Thyolo escarpment, it's a flat blue-green expanse of reeds, threaded with glinting water and dotted with nebulous shapes of palm clusters. It looks deserted, as uninhabited and mysterious as the dim bed of the sea.

Once in the valley we find that it is certainly not uninhabited. The gentle, mushroom-coloured Malawian thatching blends perfectly with the landscape and entire villages vanish easily from sight. The view too, vanishes behind a wall of tall grass and thin scattered woodland, allowing only distant views of the hazy escarpment.

The place to hire boats is James' Landing. After a few fruitless enquiries you may find that enquires for Nchacha Jemus bring better results! The road is little more than a track, but it leads to the water's edge where thirty or more dugout canoes are drawn up.

This is clearly a fishing base. Men hunker in the shade mending fishing nets. Red-gilled fish lie glinting in little heaps. Cast-off wooden floats and hand-made baked clay sinkers are strewn around. The boats themselves are a delight to the eye. Beached neatly side by side, each dugout is as individual as a fingerprint. The wood is dark and very old. All signs of the adze have long worn away; the surface is polished smooth by hands and water and weeds, and the ridges and whorls of the grain are exposed. In the scooped lip of the prow the central vortex of the heart-wood shows, and the narrow sides have knife-thin edges worn down in eccentric, almost rococo, curves and waves.

In these elderly relics of once great trees a few seconds of uncertainty coincide with adjustment to the boat's narrowness and the shifting weight of the poler behind. There is a gentle splash and hiss of the pole, a clonk as it connects with the boat, a few drops scatter as it lifts, and another soft gurgling splash. Before us are strata of bronze and green and blue, shimmering with light. The water is peat-dark and clear; a submerged lily leaf gleams amber and cornelian red through the topaz water, and mats of lime green water-cabbage bob on the surface, stiffly crimped velveteen leaves bunched in whorls. Beyond are tall sedges, then darker phragmites reed beds, and beyond again, romantic lilac hills.

A pelican faces off a rare Madagascar squacco heron

Fishermen fish in Elephant Marsh as they have done for centuries

Dragonflies play aerial skipping games above the water grass, and a squacco heron does a cloak-and-dagger stalk across the weeds. A pelican, pink and pale as frog's legs, nestles hugely among waterlilies, jacanas pertly skitter across lily pads on spread clown's feet. A pair of fulvous ducks float stem to stern, blue bills, golden cheeks and a chocolate stripe down the back of the neck, looking gilded as Cleopatra's barge. An anxious trio of black-and-white long-toed plovers chivy and scold each other. An open-billed stork stands demure in black, a sparkle of iridescence around the throat like a sequined collar. With a sudden lurch he hunches into flight, long trailing toes like lightening conductors out behind him.

A pelican circles like a Sunderland flying boat, and against the blue-green backdrop of the escarpment are dark palms in silhouette against tumbling billows of smoke. Glossy ibis probe delicately under lily pads. Between these dish-like leaves, the perfect reflection of a blue and cloud-puffed sky makes you feel you're drifting through a Monet painting. A fisherman bends a polished back, dark and lustrous as wet wood, over the hollow centre of a distant dugout. Another swings out his net like a filamented lasso, the circular splash of sound carried over open water like a special gift.

There is a hush of lily leaves against the hull, and foam froths from feathery weed compacted by the prow. Pretty rosettes of scalloped, diamond shaped leaves, each with a small basal float on the stem are water chestnuts and the fruit can be cracked with the teeth. The little nugget of fibrous white pith tastes faintly of coconut.

The elephants may have left the marsh, but crocodiles still abound. There is also the occasional hippo, though here, close to the old town of Chiromo, the land is densely populated. Despite that, and the lack of riverine forest, pink-backed pelicans can be seen nesting in a baobab tree.

A fragile platform of untidy sticks supports the unlikely bulk of two adults and a ravenous and noisy chick.

Chiromo

The ghost town of Chiromo marks the end of Elephant Marsh. This is where the rumbustious Ruo, leaping from the flanks of Mulanje, joins the slow, swampy mother river. In full flow, the Ruo dumps such volumes of water on this clogged waterway that it builds up a great ridge of water, causing the Shire to back up through the length of Elephant Marsh. In big flood years fishing villages and Chiromo itself get submerged or isolated.

Chiromo was once the major gateway to the country, home to some 300 traders and settlers. The income generated here from transport, excise and postal charges was a high proportion of the total for the entire Protectorate. It was also, of course, the base from which ivory hunters operated.

In fact the first Police and Customs Officer, Collector of Revenue and Postmaster, one Hugh Charlie Marshall, was himself a former hunter. There is a glorious photograph taken outside the first Post Office of him, slung nonchalantly in a *machila* while his gun-bearers support tusks and horns and other manly spoils from the war on wildlife.

It was Chiromo's role as gateway that made the town pivotal in Malawi's history. This was where the great battle of 1888 took place that precipitated the declaration of a Protectorate. In fact it was little more than a minor skirmish with a few Portuguese officers, but it was felt to be sufficiently threatening to have the area declared as officially under Britain's protection.

Today, across the Shire from Chiromo is the twin town Bangula, once connected by the railway line. The railway bridge still stands, but the extensive bund that carried the line beyond had a channel washed through in the floods of 1997. The dispirited line still hangs limply over the washway into the water, a sad and rusting relic.

The silt-laden Ruo, carrying much agricultural wealth in the form of topsoil, joins the Shire (left) at Chiromo

Throughout the length of the Shire crocodiles are a menace to humans and wildlife alike

A pelican at its nest near James' Landing, Elephant Marsh